PRAISE FOR

SUCCESS FACTOR X

This book reminds us all that we can make a difference and be a change agent. *Success Factor X* will inspire you to lead by example, challenge, and transform.

—**DIMITRI HALKIDIS**, president and founder of Boo2Bullying

Through the fifty amazing and diverse people featured in this book, three things are accomplished: knowledge is shared, goals seem attainable, and inspiration overflows. This book is a great example of paying it forward.

—**JAMES LOTT JR.**, host of *The SOS Show with James Lott Jr.*

I've always heard if you want to know how to succeed, hang around people who've already gotten where you want to go! I would add to that by saying, if you can't physically be where they are, read what they've written. Nowhere will you find a greater collection of highly accomplished people than in this book. It is chock-full of pearls of wisdom from some of the most successful humans on the planet! If you're looking to ignite your own passion for success, this must-read book is where you want to start!

—**TONY MCEWING**, Emmy Award–winning news anchor for *Good Day LA* and *FOX 11 Morning News*

A beautiful coffee-table tome that explores the topic of success with such joy and encouragement that it's impossible not to be moved by the stories of its participants. Their enthusiasm and inspiration is contagious, and just what our troubled world needs right now. When it comes to the Success Factor, X indeed marks the spot.

—**TOM STACY**, senior writer at *Soap Opera Digest*

It's been said that there's no secret formula to success. That may be true, but there is frank, helpful, and intelligent advice to be found in the pages of *Success Factor X: Inspiration, Wisdom, and Advice from 50 of America's Best*. This book compiles stories from myriad people who have achieved great success in unique and diverse fields. What the contributors have in common is personal stories that will inspire readers to persevere and persist until they achieve their dreams. This book doesn't preach—rather, it presents stories of success, and from those stories, the reader can feel inspired, something necessary to get through the inevitable challenging periods.

Authors Sean Kanan and Jill Liberman, who also share their journeys in this book, have assembled an impressive list of participants, including businessman/investor Mark Cuban (*Shark Tank*), Emmy-winner Susan Lucci (*All My Children*), and cosmetics mogul Dimitri James (Skinn Cosmetics).

Whether you want to own a professional sports team, perform in the arts, or create a product line doesn't really matter. The stories found in this collection are universal for anyone who wants to bring their visions to fruition and then breathe in the sweet smell of success.

Read on and become inspired to more fully live the life you've always wanted to live.

—**MICHAEL MALONEY**, author of *The Young and Restless Life of William J. Bell*

Success Factor X is this year's literary anthological compilation for the masses, webbing together fifty of the most composed and eclectic artists, actors, directors, writers, literary gurus, and entrepreneurs, in my opinion, to be assembled. The thought-provoking subjects take the reader on an otherwise unwavering journey that toggles between spirited concepts about life and life's ultimate quest and, in that, rising to the occasion when the occasion isn't necessarily handed to you.

The book's ideas reveal a collision between the potentiality of success in tandem with the recognition of subtle and sometimes unidentifiable or unannounced hardships that life will inevitably bring to us all. That being said, each page reveals the common thread of passion, drive, and tenacity that provokes one's craft to speak for itself again and again. A talking book that will definitely speak to, connect with, and provoke the masses who engage each page.

—**WILLIAM LANKFORD**, writer and editor at *Juxtapoz Art Magazine*

Success Factor X gleans wisdom directly from some of the most powerful, wealthy, and famous people in the world. Its beauty resides in its embrace of the mindset that these qualities are not what define success. It encourages you to discover a personal path to happiness and stay the course. Although it's not a road map, it provides some helpful mile markers—dozens of iterations of the words love and gratitude—for your journey.

—**JIM MERCURIO**, screenwriter, development executive, and filmmaker

INSPIRATION, WISDOM & ADVICE
FROM **50** OF AMERICA'S BEST

SUCCESS FACTOR

COMPILED BY

SEAN KANAN & JILL LIBERMAN

PLAIN SIGHT PUBLISHING | AN IMPRINT OF CEDAR FORT, INC. | SPRINGVILLE, UTAH

ISBN 13: 978-1-4621-3607-0

Published by Plain Sight Publishing, an imprint of Cedar Fort, Inc.
2373 W. 700 S., Springville, UT 84663
Distributed by Cedar Fort, Inc., www.cedarfort.com

  Library of Congress Cataloging-in-Publication Data on file.

Cover and interior design by Shawnda T. Craig and Sarah Wakefield
Cover design © 2019 Cedar Fort, Inc.
Edited and typeset by Kaitlin Barwick and Nicole Terry

Printed in China

10 9 8 7 6 5 4 3 2 1

Printed on acid-free paper

• • •

This book is dedicated to the highly accomplished actors, athletes, musicians, and industry leaders who gave their time to share what success means to them. Thank you for your inspiration, generous spirit, and insightful contributions.

We also dedicate this book to you, our readers, who share our passion for excellence and for traveling on this continuing road toward greater success.

Sean and Jill believe that an important part of success is giving back. A portion of the sale of each book is proudly being donated to the American Red Cross, a humanitarian organization that provides emergency assistance and relief to people affected by disasters across the country and around the world.

• • •

CONTENTS

CONTRIBUTORS

FOREWORD
BY JIMMY STAR

PRODUCER • DIRECTOR • AUTHOR

I n the media-driven world we're immersed in 24/7, we're constantly bombarded with the pressures to find "success"—however we choose to define it. Part of what makes this book so special, though, is the diversity of the stories within it, helping us see that there are multiple ways to succeed and diverse paths to attaining glory. From the comic timing of Jason Alexander to Harry Wayne Casey, the disco pioneer who created KC and the Sunshine Band, from boxing promoter Don King and his historic matchups in the ring to the historic prowess of investor Mark Cuban—*Success Factor X* presents us with stimulating stories of what success can be.

What does being successful mean to you? This book will help you ponder your own personal answer to the question we're continually faced with, starting in early childhood. We continually have the chance to consider the role models of success in our lives—starting with the parents, teachers, and friends we're exposed to as we each grow up.

But just because we eventually become adults who live with the choices we make within our lives doesn't mean we have to cease asking ourselves the question "What success do I want to strive for here and now?" The beauty of this book is the opportunity to consider and learn from a wide variety of achievers in their fields. Who knows? Reading about and learning from the attainments of these celebrated leaders might confirm that you have chosen the right path to your own success . . . or stimulate you to consider new definitions or permutations of your own goals for success.

I know that my own ideas of success have evolved with my place in the world. My career in the fashion and entertainment industries has been filled with challenges, hardships, and amazing achievements. I'm grateful for all of that and even for the trials and tribulations along the way that forced me to learn, change, and grow.

I've found myself shifting lanes along the way—from beginning my adult life as a celebrity clothing designer, working with my favorite actors and actresses in the world of entertainment, to becoming the host of *The Jimmy Star Show with Ron Russell*, which has become the number-one webshow in the world, with 4.5 million weekly viewers and listeners. I was honored to be named the fifth most influential radio personality to follow on social media and the best entertainment publicist in the United States. Those were all gratifying successes, but what I've found for myself is that the taste of one success can breed the desire for still more and different ones.

For me that's meant perpetually pushing myself to find and confront challenges I hadn't yet pursued . . . even if they took me a bit out of my comfort zone at first. The desire to taste new successes is what led me to become a best-selling author, writing several fiction and nonfiction books. My plans have continued to evolve and change over the years—not always by choice, but always with the adrenaline that comes from being immersed in new situations and contexts.

I always strive to keep moving forward, going through the doors that have opened but always looking out for new pathways into the future. I've found that it's important to savor each experience—good or bad—to learn from every one of them.

I feel fortunate and blessed to have been asked to participate in writing this foreword to *Success Factor X*. That's partly because of my deep admiration for Jill Liberman and Sean Kanan. In my own honest opinion, these two have created one of the most unique books ever written, giving us each the opportunity to learn from a wide range of extremely talented and successful individuals. All of these contributors have excelled in their career choices, and each represents the epitome of "success" in his or her field.

Certainly, that's true of the pair who have brought us this special collection of wise perspectives. Jill Liberman continues to succeed in all of her endeavors—as a motivational speaker, published author, television executive, and radio host, all of which have led her to be featured as one of the most inspirational women in America. Sharing Jill's journey and her ideas of success in this book as well as in her work as a motivational speaker expands our idea of what it can mean to be successful.

The same must be said of Sean Kanan—an incredible actor, producer, and writer. After long ago becoming a huge fan of *The Karate Kid* film series, I eventually realized that I had become his fan for life, continuing over the years to follow his ever-increasing personal and professional accomplishments. As our two careers began to flourish, Sean and I crossed paths in person when he did a guest appearance on the webshow I mentioned earlier. We very soon learned that our viewers and listeners were mesmerized by Sean's knowledge, playfulness, down-to-earth personality, and humanity. He's a genuine success in many varied ways, working diligently to give back while sharing his experiences and contributing to the world we all live in.

I bet you'll find as I have that it's quite stimulating to read the collected thoughts and ideas of remarkably accomplished icons in the worlds of sports, music, entertainment, and business. All of these contributors have reached the pinnacle of their fields, yet they continue to amaze with their ongoing successes and accomplishments.

When reading the list of *Success Factor X* contributors, I was astounded, excited, and intrigued to see how everyone involved described their own ideas of success . . . but always gave us something of takeaway value to consider for ourselves. I've had the privilege to meet, interview, and work with many of the contributors of this amazing book throughout my career, and I'm impressed by the sheer quality of the achievers sharing their perspectives.

I believe that as you read *Success Factor X*, you'll find insights, knowledge, and ideas to help you define and pursue your personal journey to success. Part of the magic of the book is the ability to learn from so many different kinds of very successful people and, with each new story, to consider advice that can help you as individuals define *your* goals for success and the path that *you* plan to pursue in achieving it.

Big congrats, in closing, to Jill Liberman and Sean Kanan for writing and assembling this compilation from so many exceptional icons in their fields. They have done a service for us all. Wherever you are right now on your particular journey through life, this book offers valuable perspectives. Read it slowly and with an open mind. Savor the information provided, discover what works for you, and take action on your own road to success.

—Jimmy Star

Jimmy Star is the host of *The Jimmy Star Show with Ron Russell*, the number-one celebrity interview webshow (TV and radio) in the world, with 4.5 million weekly viewers and listeners. He is an influencer in entertainment and ranks in the top 1 percent of all social media users in the world. Jimmy Star was recently named the fifth most influential radio personality in the world to follow in social media, and he is an award-winning publicist, recently named Publicist of the Year in both the Nashville Universe Music Awards and the Kdub Hit Country music awards for 2018.

He is an accomplished author and is also the celebrity who interviews celebrities for *Stars and Celebs* (previously *The Celebrity Café*), the oldest celebrity news website in the world, and is also a major contributor for *The Hollywood Digest*.

ACKNOWLEDGMENTS

JILL

Success is surrounding yourself with people you
like being with and who lift you up.

To Stan Shanbron: Thank you for your constant encouragement,
unconditional love, and never-ending support.

To Adam and Kristen: Thank you for the joy and happiness you
add to my life and for making me proud every day.

To Sean: Thanks for never making a day of this wonderful project feel like work.

SEAN

To Michele: My best friend, my love, my everything.

To my family: Thank you for your love, support, and infinite patience.

To Sensei William Stoner: Thank you for helping me
discover the courage to follow my dreams.

To Peter Kanan: For your continuous help and support.

To Jill: Thank you for being a kindred spirit and joining me on this adventure.

JILL AND SEAN

To Bryce and the publishing team at Cedar Fort: Thank you for
sharing our vision and believing in us and this project.

INTRODUCTION

Sean is an internationally known actor as well as an author and producer. Jill is an impassioned motivational speaker and author. They live to inspire, and they love their work. They met in 2004 when Sean participated in Jill's book *American Pride*.

Sean recently hit a milestone birthday, and Jill called to send him good wishes. The conversation soon led us to brainstorming about our mutual desire to reach people on a large scale in a meaningful way. By the end of the call, we were writing partners. We share a desire to work on projects that have passion and purpose, and we thought of the idea to compile a positive, motivational book on success.

Our writing serves as a conduit to reaching others. We knew that a book would be an effective and powerful medium to convey our message. Recognizing that we live in a society often driven by division rather than unity, we wanted to champion a project devoted to a theme shared by all. We selected the topic of success. We contacted accomplished celebrities, athletes, musicians, and business leaders and asked them to discuss in their own words what success means to them, what advice they have received on their journey, and what advice they have to offer. Everyone has his or her own definition of success. The idea to gather an impressive group of trusted and incredible success stories and offer their thoughts on one platform excites us because it allows us to help people have access to and learn from leaders who have achieved so much. We reached out to America's most famous and collected their favorite tips, personal stories, and heartfelt advice to help provide that insight to the world. What better way to tackle the subject than go straight to the high achievers who most would describe as "having it all"—money, power, and fame? You may be surprised to learn that none of our contributors define their success in those terms. Much of the joy in assembling this project comes from the knowledge that our contributors have the passion and willingness to share the stories and secrets of their successes.

Society has a preoccupation with celebrities, pop culture, and the pursuit of success. There is no shortage of autobiographical success books. How is *Success Factor X* unique? Most notably, it is not a business book on what it takes to be successful. Rather, it showcases highly accomplished people sharing tips and advice based on their lives and personal journeys. This book has a wonderful hybrid nature combining a coffee table format with insight and inspiration. *Success Factor X* is not *about* accomplished people—it is *by* accomplished people. Our book has original content provided directly from the participants. This upbeat compilation of the advice from fifty successful people is a quick read and can be referred to often.

Some passages are short and simple, and some more detailed. This book draws its strength from the eclectic and diverse participants who universally share similar views of what success is and how it is achieved. With such a varied group of contributors, *Success Factor X* highlights someone relatable and of interest to any reader: a famous pioneer of rap, a transgender actor and advocate for the LGBTQ community, an Italian prince, an Olympic champion, and numerous professional athletes, television stars, business icons, music moguls, and self-made billionaires representing different ages, genders, and ethnic backgrounds. Readers from all walks of life will benefit from the wisdom, inspiration, and battle-tested advice revealed in *Success Factor X*.

This project represents a labor of love. We are truly grateful for the success that we have achieved and for the opportunity we have to give back. It is our hope that this book will encourage you to define success in new and varied ways. Success can be daunting. We all experience challenges, struggles, and disappointments. This is our way to pay it forward and remind you that you can accomplish and become anything. We are proud to donate a portion from the sale of each book to the American Red Cross, the world's preeminent humanitarian organization providing emergency assistance and disaster relief wherever needed.

Learn from and be motivated by some of America's best. However you define success, we know this book will inspire you to believe that anything is possible with determination and the right attitude. Look deep within yourself, define your goals, take action, and never quit.

To your success!

—Jill and Sean

SUCCESS
ALWAYS DEMANDS

— A —

greater

EFFORT

WINSTON CHURCHILL

JASON ALEXANDER

ACTOR • COMEDIAN • DIRECTOR

S ome of the most seemingly successful people I have known have also been desperately unhappy or unfulfilled. **Success is not comparative—it is personal. Your success is defined by you.** And it is best understood and measured by those you care about. Set a goal, go for the goal, assess your achievement. Then set another goal. Did you do what you wanted to do? If not, why? What can you improve? Were you surprised, pleasantly or not, along the way? Who else did you affect? How was your journey for them?

SOME OF THE THINGS I CONSIDER MOST SUCCESSFUL IN MY LIFE WERE NOT THE BIGGEST OR MOST LAUDED.

Some of them were considered failures by others. But using these questions I have posed, I feel I am one of the most successful and blessed people in the world. Size, popularity, superlatives, rewards—these are not always the best measure of success. They are merely indicators of how much your personal success has affected others. But I can tell you that it is possible to achieve all those without feeling personally invested or successful. It is a hollow achievement.

MEASURE YOUR SUCCESS FROM WITHIN. IT IS THE TRUEST MEASURE YOU HAVE. AND IF IT MEASURES UP, REJOICE.

Though best known for his award-winning, nine-year stint as the now-iconic George Costanza of television's *Seinfeld*, Jason Alexander has achieved international recognition for a career noted for its extraordinary diversity. Aside from his performances on stage, screen, and television, he has worked extensively as a writer, composer, director, producer, and teacher of acting. In between all that, he has also become an award-winning magician, a notorious poker player, and a respected advocate on social and political issues.

For his depiction of George on *Seinfeld*, Jason garnered six Emmy nominations, four Golden Globe nominations, an American Television Award, and two American Comedy Awards. He won two Screen Actor Guild Awards as the best actor in a television comedy, despite playing a supporting role, and in 2012, he was honored to receive the Julie Harris Award for Lifetime Achievement from the Actors Fund.

Jason starred in the television films of *Bye Bye Birdie*, *Cinderella*, *A Christmas Carol*, and *The Man Who Saved Christmas*. Additionally, his voice has been heard most notably in *Duckman*, *The Cleveland Show*, *American Dad*, *Tom and Jerry*, and *Kody Kapow*. He can also be heard in the upcoming animated series *Harley Quinn*.

He directed the feature films *For Better or Worse* and *Just Looking*. He is also a distinguished television director and won the American Country Music Award for his direction of Brad Paisley's video "Cooler Online."

Mr. Alexander tours the country and the world performing his one-man show, "As Long as You're Asking—A Conversation with Jason Alexander," which contains music, comedy, and conversation.

The
MAN OF VIRTUE
makes the
**DIFFICULTY TO
BE OVERCOME**
his first business, and
SUCCESS
only a subsequent
consideration.

—Confucius

BRAD ARNOLD

FOUNDER AND LEAD SINGER OF 3 DOORS DOWN

am still learning what success is. When I first started performing in front of huge crowds, everyone cheering us on, I thought that was success, and I suppose in some ways it was—selling records, playing sold-out shows, and making good money. That had to be what it was all about. **However, those were simply the seeds of success, and I'd mistaken them for the harvest.** True success is actually hearing the stories and learning what the songs we'd created meant to the people that listened to them. It was finding out what we'd all gleaned from the music that we'd created. Success was and is found in hearing about how a song helped someone through a hard time, helped them remember a celebrated moment, or helped them remember a person that is gone.

SUCCESS IS KNOWING THAT IN YOUR OWN WAY, YOU CHANGED YOUR PORTION OF THE STORY FOR THE BETTER.

As a singer, songwriter, and founder of the multi-platinum rock band 3 Doors Down, Brad Arnold's prolific career has spanned the globe. Since 3 Doors Down's formation in 1995 with Brad's childhood friends in Mississippi, the band has sold more than twenty million albums and garnered three Grammy nominations, two American Music Awards, and five BMI Pop Awards for songwriting, including BMI's coveted Songwriter of the Year award. When Brad isn't on the road, you can find him taking care of his sixty-acre working horse farm. Brad and his wife, Jen, live outside of Nashville, Tennessee.

CORBIN BERNSEN

ACTOR • PRODUCER • DIRECTOR

SUCCESS. AH! CHASING THE RABBIT ...

That's how I've always viewed success: engaging, disengaging, wins and losses . . . all fleeting. But that healthy view has given me the fiber to continue, realizing that success isn't "the thing." Rather, it's a byproduct of a conceptualization, a goal, and then implementation and integration of it through study, then a plan, followed by an all-out effort to "get there."

What I realized early on, however—thanks, Mom—is that **"getting there" isn't "success"** as we know it. Instead, success is based on the vast achievements we earned on the way to our goal—life's lessons, what you do with and make of your life while it's actually happening. I've traveled across our great country by car often, always with the destination—East or West Coast—in mind too. Successful trips, however, were never based on the speed in which I reached my destination or even on the requirement that I reached them at all.

A SUCCESSFUL TRIP HAS ALWAYS BEEN TIED TO THE STOPS ALONG THE WAY, THE DISCOVERY OF NEW NATURAL WONDERS, NEW TOWNS, AND NEW FOODS, AND THE PEOPLE I'VE CROSSED PATHS WITH.

I'm sixty-three now, and while I don't play the ageism card when it comes to acting and "Hollywood," the reality is that there are simply fewer parts for older actors. This is a reflection of life—how many grandparents are at the table vs. the kids? And great stories, for the most part, focus on that glorious age of discovery where we are learning, falling in love for the first time, and suffering our first wins and our first losses. Of course there are fantastic stories (I write about them in particular) about our "aging fleet" and the battles we've won and lost, the new challenges and our impending demises, but the audience is smaller for that kind of meal, and that's okay. I digress . . .

THE POINT HERE IS THAT I APPRECIATE THE ROAD OF MY CAREER AND LIFE, AND I BASE WHAT I SEE AS "SUCCESS" ON THAT JOURNEY RATHER THAN "GETTING SOMEWHERE."

This is what continues to fuel me, burns a fire in me, and in turn, makes me feel successful. Continually! My world continues to appreciate the past abundance of both deadly curves and vistas of extraordinary beauty and awe and remains excited about the new ones just over the horizon.

I openly admit that I'm the greyhound chasing the mechanical rabbit toward the next hill, empowered by what I've experienced and driven by what's next . . . that and taking in every inch of the road along the way.

THAT'S SUCCESS!
A LIFE GAINED, NOTHING LOST.

A graduate of UCLA, Bernsen earned a master's degree in playwriting but continues to jump between all mediums, excited to explore the endless possibilities to tell a story.

His career began with the NBC TV series *L.A. Law*. Along the way, he hosted *Saturday Night Live* and guest-starred on *Seinfeld* and *Star Trek*, to name a few notable television appearances. Most currently, he starred on USA Network's series *Psych* and Starz's *American Gods* and can be seen in Netflix's *The Punisher*. Corbin's film roles include *Disorganized Crime*, *Shattered*, *Tales from the Hood*, *Kiss Kiss Bang Bang*, and *Major League*.

On the other side of the camera, he wrote and directed the films *Dead Air*, *Rust*, and *25 Hill* and recently released *Life with Dog*.

With his wife of thirty years, Amanda Pays, he recently relocated to the Hudson Valley, New York, remodeled a farmhouse, and has begun writing the play *American Executions*, about the first live televised public executions.

ALL OUR

Dreams

CAN COME TRUE
IF WE HAVE THE

Courage

TO PURSUE THEM.

Walt Disney

SARA BLAKELY

FOUNDER AND CEO OF SPANX

T hink about what success looks like to you. Get a specific mental picture. Are you standing on a balcony in your dream home looking out over the ocean? Are you talking with world leaders? **Before I started SPANX, I saw myself on a stage, talking with Oprah.** I didn't know what we were talking about, but that was my mental snapshot of success. And then I spent the next fifteen years filling in the blanks, trying to figure out what Oprah and I were talking about on that stage. When it finally arrived, I never dreamed I would be talking about a new type of undergarment I invented.

TRUSTING MY GUT, BELIEVING IN MY PRODUCT, AND NOT BEING AFRAID TO FAIL WERE CRUCIAL TO THE SUCCESS OF SPANX.

I heard "no" a million times but persevered because I knew I had created a product that would change the way women get dressed.

As long as I can remember, I have felt compelled to help women. When I signed The Giving Pledge, I pledged to invest in women because I believe it offers one of the greatest returns on investment.

WITH A LITTLE SUPPORT, WOMEN PAY FORWARD SUCCESS TO THEIR FAMILIES AND COMMUNITIES.

For me, it's most fulfilling to see the ripples turn into waves when women are empowered to fulfill their potential.

Sara Blakely is the founder and CEO of SPANX, Inc. The dynamic women's brand has revolutionized an industry and changed the way women around the world get dressed. SPANX is known for inventing smarter, more comfortable must-haves for women, including bras, leggings, activewear, undies, Arm Tights™, and of course their famous shapewear, which creates the perfect smooth canvas under clothes. Sara was selected as one of *Time* magazine's 100 Most Influential People and has been featured on the covers of magazines like *Forbes, Inc., Success,* and *Atlanta.* In support of her mission to empower women, Sara created the SPANX by Sara Blakely Foundation in 2006, and in 2013, she signed The Giving Pledge, committing to donate half of her wealth to charity. Sara and her family reside in Atlanta, Georgia. Sara is a native of Clearwater, Florida, and a graduate of Florida State University.

I HAVE NOT FAILED.

I've just found

10,000

ways that

WON'T WORK.

• Thomas Edison •

JAMES CULLEN BRESSACK

DIRECTOR • PRODUCER

Success is all relative. I have never considered myself to be a successful person—I am just a workaholic. I am constantly hard on myself, forcing myself to work nonstop. I am always grateful for the opportunities I have been given. I am never complacent being where I am. I always want to be something bigger and better, to continue to grow.

I feel the only recipe for success is to not focus on being successful. If you spend too much time believing your own hype, you will never become what you want to be. Don't talk—go out there and *do*. I wanted to be a filmmaker, so I went out there and picked up a camera. Always work hard for what you want, and don't give up. The only difference between you and the person you want to be like is that person didn't give up.

Without failure, there is no success. To succeed you have to fail. You have to fail miserably. You have to experience that and know what that's like. Because once you do, if you choose to keep fighting, you will do everything you can to never be in that place again.

There's never enough time to do everything right, but there's always time to do it again.

ALWAYS RISE TO THE OCCASION.

James Cullen Bressack has been called "horror's new hope" and "a talent to watch out for." His first film reached the top of the best sellers list on Amazon in the horror category. Bressack made history with his feature *To Jennifer*, which was the first feature film shot entirely on an iPhone 5. He followed with seven features, including *Pernicious*, *13-13-13*, *If Looks Could Kill*—which aired on *Lifetime* and *LMN*—and *Blood Lake*—which aired on *Animal Planet* and was top rated. After writing and directing *Bethany*, a horror film that generated rave reviews, James focused his time on producing. After producing many films, two of which were released by Lionsgate and one by Cinedigm, he joined the PGA (Producers Guild of America) and is currently a proud member. One of James's recent producing efforts was ranked number fourteen in the weekly top charts of DVD and Blu-ray sales of all films in the country. He has won multiple Best Picture and Best Director awards on the film festival circuit. Aside from his new ventures in virtual reality, James recently directed *Cargo*, an animated feature film.

BOBBI BROWN

FOUNDER OF BOBBI BROWN COSMETICS •
AUTHOR • ENTREPRENEUR

When I was younger, I believed that success meant that you made a lot of money, had a good job, got married, and had kids. At the time, I aspired to somehow make $100,000 a year. I know now that success has less to do with making money and has a lot to do with being happy: **loving your job, being in a great marriage, and having wonderful kids.**

I FEEL INCREDIBLY GRATEFUL TO THE UNIVERSE FOR THE SUCCESS I'VE HAD, AND I HAVE REALLY LEARNED TO APPRECIATE IT.

Baseball legend Yogi Berra, for example, was a good friend of mine who always said, **"You can observe a lot from watching."** As a kid, I watched Papa Sam, who came over from Russia and created his business with a lot of hard work. From him, I learned that persistence is key. My parents taught me so much too. From my mom, I learned that people are the same wherever you go. My dad ignited in me passion and creativity—he always encouraged me to go outside of my comfort zone. Later in life, he taught me how to keep it all in check by compartmentalizing.

Successfully starting a business and then selling it is something not a lot of people get to do. In hindsight, it's so awesome, so incredible, and I feel so very grateful starting round two from nothing all over again. I am creating an indie, entrepreneurial lifestyle brand, and at the same time, **I am teaching and learning from the people I work with.**

AND I AM NOT AFRAID OF FAILURE—IT ONLY MEANS THAT I SHOULD BE DOING SOMETHING ELSE.

Bobbi Brown is a beauty industry titan, world-renowned makeup artist, best-selling author, sought-after speaker, and serial entrepreneur. Bobbi has written nine beauty and wellness books, and as a professional makeup artist, she created ten simple lipsticks that evolved into a global beauty empire. In 1995, the eponymously named Bobbi Brown Cosmetics was acquired by The Estée Lauder Companies, where Bobbi served as Chief Creative Officer, building a billion-dollar brand. In October 2016, she left the company in order to launch Beauty Evolution LLC.

Bobbi has returned to her roots as an entrepreneur. Her latest endeavor, EVOLUTION_18, is a line of lifestyle-inspired wellness products that launched in the spring of 2018. In addition, Bobbi and her husband, Steven Plofker, have recently opened The George, a boutique hotel with thirty-two lovingly reimagined rooms in Montclair, New Jersey.

BE IT jewel OR toy,
NOT THE PRIZE
GIVES THE joy,
BUT THE STRIVING
TO WIN THE prize.
— EDWARD BULWER-LYTTON —

KIMBERLIN BROWN

ACTRESS • ENTREPRENEUR

Success means many things to different people. **For me, it means taking risks that others are afraid of.** Success means failing sometimes multiple times before succeeding. We can only achieve our personal level of greatness by trying. **Please don't let anyone tell you that you can't!** *Can't* never did anything, as my mother would say. **We are ALL capable**; we just have to put ourselves out there and risk failure, stare it in the face, and succeed.

THERE ARE THOSE AROUND YOU WHO ARE MOST WILLING TO HELP. OPEN YOUR EYES AND SEE THEM.

Kimberlin Pelzer Brown has spent the past three decades building a multifaceted career in business, philanthropy, entertainment, and agriculture. While she is best known for her prominent role in CBS's award-winning international soap operas, she is also a proud wife and mother, successful entrepreneur, philanthropist, two-time bone marrow donor, and passionate advocate for women in politics. She was a prime-time featured speaker at the Republican National Convention in 2016 and a 2018 congressional candidate.

STEVE BURTON

ACTOR • FITNESS COACH •
FOUNDER OF BURTON NUTRITION

My grandfather Jack Burton was instrumental in laying some of the foundations of success. He was a master door-to-door salesman for Electrolux. When I was younger, I would visit him around the holidays, and he would have me write down my goals for the next year, then put them in an envelope and seal it. I was twelve years old, and, sure enough, things on that list would materialize. His work ethic was like no other, and he passed that down to me. He said, **"I may not be the smartest guy in the room, but I'll outwork any of them. I knock on more doors."** Grandpa Burton's last piece of advice was actually how he signed his letters to me:

K.I.S.S. *KEEP IT SIMPLE, STUPID.*

Nothing holds truer today for me when I'm making decisions.

When I was growing up, my dad wasn't around until later, and my uncle Mike Burton was a huge positive influence. He was always there for me. I saw how hard he worked and how he took care of everybody. He had a servant's heart, which I feel is important for a successful entrepreneur, and he taught me to just do the right thing.

When I started my acting career, I was really introduced to failure and disappointment. It wasn't failure due to lack of trying, that's for sure. I started when I was sixteen, so I owe a lot to my dad for always being positive no matter the situation. He would say, "Hey kid, it's just a numbers game. Next time." In theory, he was right. My dad was a great influence, always telling me I could achieve anything if I put my mind to it. I learned perseverance and consistency. I am fortunate, even though I had parents who were divorced and I grew up in not the greatest of circumstances, my mom and dad always encouraged me. I believe this is a big part of why I have success. There are obviously other components that lead to success, but **I feel the biggest killer, the anti-success formula, is negativity and negative people.** I try to avoid "it" and people who are stuck in a negative place at all costs. **They will take your soul. Run.**

I've been blessed to work with a lot of great actors and directors. At any job, I would gravitate toward the people who were successful and try to learn from them. The genre didn't matter; from daytime to big-budget features, there were some common themes: **show up on time,**

know your lines, work hard, and be nice to people. I just had my twenty-seventh anniversary in daytime, and I still abide by this daily. When I first started out, I was searching for mentors without really knowing it. Actually, Sean Kanan, who is the coauthor of this book, was one of them. He helped me with a lot of things in life, but most important, he guided me toward a financial advisor and showed me how to take care of my money. **There are lessons to learn from others who paved the way.**

I've always had an entrepreneurial spirit, which means I've had successes and failures. I've been fortunate to have more wins than losses, but those losses and those failures are just as important as the wins.

THE TRUTH IS, THE FAILURES HURT, BUT THE FAILURES HAVE MADE ME WHO I AM.

The hardest thing to do is embrace a failure. We are not wired that way, but in my experience, sometimes great things come out of being uncomfortable. It makes us reflect and grow. If you ain't growing, you ain't going. Personal growth is a key. Start sooner than later. I love Thomas Edison's quote **"I have not failed. I have just found ten thousand ways that won't work."** Talk about turning failures into lessons and never quitting.

The one thing I wish I had done sooner is learn how to control my day. What does this mean? I'm a big proponent of setting yourself up for success, and as an entrepreneur, you'll have to sacrifice things to succeed. So I feel that controlling the start of my day is a key to my success. In a nutshell, I get up, I hydrate, I drink a cup of coffee, I listen to a mentor or leader, I work out, I shower, I pray, I'm grateful, and then I visualize my goals. I do some sort of version of this daily. I feel energized, and then I can attack my day instead of being on the defense. Health and fitness are important to me. I believe having a healthy mind and body sets me up for success and helps me grind it out when the going gets tough.

What advice would I give? Well, I tell my kids to "Believe and Achieve" and to K.I.S.S.

LOVE WHAT YOU DO, AND WE'LL FIGURE OUT HOW TO MAKE MONEY AT IT.

You will have to **"do what others don't to achieve or have what others won't,"** and no one can stop you from achieving your dreams.

Stay humble, be grateful, set your goals, write them down, visualize them, take extraordinary action toward them, serve others, and never give up, because there will be times when you want to. Keep the faith. Go the extra mile. Don't be afraid to ask for help. Have a good support system and mentors.

My wife, Sheree, is amazing and supportive. She's less of a risk taker, and that balances out my "jump off a cliff and figure out how to make a parachute on the way down" mentality. We are a great team.

IN SHORT, I'VE BEEN BLESSED WITH AN INCREDIBLE WIFE AND AMAZING KIDS, AND I GET TO DO WHAT I LOVE TO DO EVERY DAY. THAT'S SUCCESS TO ME.

Steve Burton is a two-time Emmy Award–winning actor, fitness coach, and successful entrepreneur. As a television and film actor and director, he is best known for his work on *General Hospital*, DreamWorks's *The Last Castle* with Robert Redford and James Gandolfini, *The Young and the Restless*, *Out of This World*, and Steven Spielberg's Emmy-winning miniseries *Taken* and for voicing the Cloud Strife character in the *Final Fantasy* video game and movie franchise.

Steve is an entrepreneur at heart. Outside of acting, he has invested and partnered in multiple businesses in a variety of industries, including finance, entertainment, real estate, restaurants, and nightlife.

Most recently, Steve launched a family business and longtime dream: Burton Nutrition. With a huge passion for health and fitness, Steve and his wife, Sheree, want to inspire people to live healthier and be their best.

Steve and Sheree enjoy life in Southern California with their three kids.

HARRY WAYNE "KC" CASEY

FOUNDER AND LEAD SINGER OF
KC AND THE SUNSHINE BAND

FOLLOW YOUR HEART.

Everything you do in life is like a ladder to get to your goal—always take steps up.

IT'S OKAY TO HOLD ON A STEP, BUT NEVER TAKE A STEP DOWN.

Harry Wayne Casey, the founder and lead singer of KC and the Sunshine Band, has been called the Founder of the Dance Revolution. KC's music has been featured at every major sporting event in the world, including the Super Bowl; World Series; Conference Championships; the NBA; Collegiate Bowl Games; National Championship Games; the NASCAR racing circuit and championships; The World Cup; The Indianapolis 500; The Kentucky Derby; *every* holiday parade, including the famous Macy's Thanksgiving Parade and the Tournament of Roses Parade; political party conventions; and presidential campaigns. The band has also been featured on more than two hundred motion picture film soundtracks.

The music originated with humble beginnings in Hialeah, Florida. KC and the Sunshine Band became the first act to score four number-one pop singles in one 12-month period since the Beatles in 1964. Three of those singles crossed over to become number-one R&B singles as well. KC's third album, *Part 3*, released in 1976, also went triple platinum and contained the number-one singles "I'm Your Boogie Man," "Shake Your Booty," and "Keep It Comin' Love."

He received Grammy Awards for Album of the Year as well as Producer of the Year in 1978 for his work on the *Saturday Night Fever* soundtrack. In 2001, KC was honored with the NARAS Governor's Award, the highest honor given by a chapter of the Academy. In 2002, KC received a coveted star on the Hollywood Walk of Fame.

KC's music is now being sampled by rappers, and whole new generations of fans have been introduced to his music. KC and the Sunshine Band have been entertaining audiences around the world for over thirty-seven years and have sold in excess of 100 million records—and that's the way they like it. Uh-huh uh-huh!

CINDY COWAN

TELEVISION AND FILM PRODUCER

uccess is about setting a goal and then taking steps to achieve it. **Don't just talk about it—do something to go out and achieve it.** Take the necessary steps. Don't judge *your* personal success on the level of what others have accomplished. Everybody holds a different meaning of the word *success*. To some, it's a dollar value, to others, it's about accomplishments, and for some, it's about helping people and leaving a legacy.

TO BE TRULY SUCCESSFUL MEANS BEING HAPPY ON A DAILY BASIS AND MAKING OTHERS HAPPY IN RETURN.

Cindy Cowan cofounded Initial Entertainment Group (IEG) in 1995, which became the leading film production and foreign sales company. Before its sale to Splendid Films in 2000, IEG had many successes, including an Emmy nomination, Golden Globe and People's Choice nominations, and a United Nations Award. Since then, Cindy has formed a new production company, Cindy Cowan Entertainment. Ms. Cowan has produced several films, including *Scorched*, starring Woody Harrelson and Alicia Silverstone, and has executive produced *Fifty Dead Men Walking*, starring Sir Ben Kingsley.

Cindy sits on the boards of Little Kids Rock, a nonprofit organization that provides free instruments and lessons to underserved public schools, and Children Mending Hearts, a dynamic arts-based enrichment education program that helps empower disadvantaged youth, building empathy and global citizenry.

Cindy Cowan is a graduate of Tulane University, with graduate courses toward a master's degree in psychology at Harvard. Cowan is also a major equestrian, winning the World Champion title more than five times in American Saddlebred five-gaited and equestrian horses.

MARK CUBAN

"SHARK" ON ABC'S *SHARK TANK* • OWNER OF THE DALLAS MAVERICKS • ENTREPRENEUR

TO ME, THE DEFINITION OF SUCCESS IS WAKING UP WITH A SMILE ON YOUR FACE KNOWING IT'S GOING TO BE A GREAT DAY.

Mark is chairman and CEO of AXS TV, one of ABC's "sharks" on the hit show *Shark Tank*, and an investor in an ever-growing portfolio of businesses.

From the age of twelve, Mark has been a natural businessman. Selling garbage bags door to door in his youth planted the seed early on for what would eventually become long-term success. After graduating from Indiana University, Mark moved to Dallas. He created MicroSolutions, a computer consulting service that was sold in 1990 to CompuServe.

In 1995, Mark and long-time friend Todd Wagner came up with an internet-based solution to not being able to listen to Hoosiers basketball games out in Texas. That solution was Broadcast.com—streaming audio over the internet. In just four years, Broadcast.com (then AudioNet) sold to Yahoo for $5.6 billion.

Since his acquisition of the Dallas Mavericks in 2000, Mark has overseen the Mavs compete in the NBA Finals for the first time in franchise history in 2006 and become NBA World Champions in 2011. They are currently listed as one of *Forbes*'s most valuable franchises in sports.

FUMIO DEMURA
MARTIAL ARTS CHAMPION

When it comes to the idea of success, I have been extremely fortunate in my life in every way possible. Publicly, I am most recognized in the world of martial arts and in the martial arts elements of movie-making. The single most well known of my contributions is as the stunt/fighting double and character element inspiration for the beloved Mr. Miyagi character of the first four *Karate Kid* movies. Over the years, I have been most grateful for the privilege of bringing happiness to the many people who have enjoyed my work, not only in the limelight, but even more important, in working with martial arts students and organizations in dojos, seminars, and competitions all over the world.

What is the "secret" to my success? First was my very great fortune to have parents who taught me the essential truths about life:

PEOPLE ARE THE MOST IMPORTANT PART OF LIFE, AND HARD WORK IS THE ONLY WAY TO ACHIEVE YOUR GOALS.

Everything else comes after those two truths. Believe me, I am not saying the path is easy, but the way is abundantly clear—care about people and work as hard as you can. Of course, many other elements are important to the recipe as well, such as being willing to be innovative, keeping a sharp eye out for opportunities, and **always, always getting up after you've fallen.**

Caring about people helps you develop friendships and working associations and motivates you to be a good and helpful friend, coworker, or any other kind of relationship you can have with the people around you. Not only does this enrich your life with deep friendships and relationships, but it also brings you opportunities that might not otherwise come your way. Today, it seems to me that people look for the opportunities before they've developed the relationships, and as a result, they are often disappointed. However, I believe that underneath any new trend in our society, **developing solid and trusting relationships with other people is both a joy of its own and also one of the greatest resources a person can have in life.** I can't count the number of times a friend or associate thought of me and brought an opportunity to me that was both totally unexpected and ultimately very successful. This was my path to Mr. Miyagi.

HARD WORK IS A VERY INTERESTING IDEA.

I've often found that people can think they are working hard, but in reality, they are not actually applying themselves with a clear mind. They don't focus on making sure their fundamentals are solid. They can think they are beyond fundamentals, but in truth, *nobody* is beyond fundamentals. People often seem to think they have **"done enough"** to get where they want to go, when in actuality **they have fallen far short of applying the amount and focus of effort needed to attain their goals**, and they end up disappointed. When I failed my first karate test, I immediately understood that I had to take responsibility for myself and that my only course was to work hard with a clear focus on fundamentals and on the steps to attaining my goals. This was my path to my place in martial arts.

I continue to try to achieve goals in my life, to cherish the people around me, and to work hard. I continue to try to be the best person I can be and to help my students to become the best people they can be . . . **and that is the true secret to my success.**

Shihan Fumio Demura is one of the most knowledgeable of martial arts masters in the world. His expertise is in the techniques of innumerable arts and styles, although he is best known for Japanese Shito-Ryu Karate-Do. He also develops training and competition in weapons (Kobudo) and sword (Batto-Do and Lai-Do). Mr. Demura is exceptional for his drive to introduce martial arts to people of all ages throughout the world. His countless contributions have earned him the love and respect of people everywhere. His dedication to benefiting as many lives as possible keeps Mr. Demura at the forefront of the martial arts arena.

Logic
WILL GET
YOU FROM

A TO B.

Imagination

WILL TAKE YOU

EVERYWHERE.

Albert Einstein

JAY DOBYNS

RETIRED UNDERCOVER ATF AGENT • AUTHOR

You **outwork your competition.** You grind and persevere. "Resiliency" becomes your middle name. You are tough and smart, and you treat people the right way . . . and you don't receive what you deserve. You are denied what you are owed. You're lying in the dirt, bleeding, beaten, defeated, pathetic. Take a moment. Calm yourself. Then get up and punch yourself in the mouth to remind yourself nothing is fair. There is no such thing. **Being deserving does not mean you are owed.**

SUCCESS COMES TO THOSE WHO FAIL AND THEN FAIL AGAIN BUT REFUSE TO BE CONQUERED.

Our best lessons are learned when we fall short, but only when we rise and endure and continue. Nothing I ever accomplished came easy. I never reached any goal entirely on my own. I raged back against all the obstacles and embraced those who were willing to move me forward. In the end, triumph over tragedy and celebration of your accomplishment with credit given to God and others brings **a joy and satisfaction that no amount of money, no trophy, no award can match.**

Jay Dobyns was a federal agent for twenty-seven years before retiring in 2014. He achieved worldwide notoriety as one of history's most daring undercover operators during high-octane missions targeting America's violent crime.

A defense attorney once described Jay as "a government-trained 'Predator' repeatedly sent on seek and destroy missions in search of drugs, guns and violence, with instructions to succeed at any cost and without regard for the agent himself or those he crosses paths with."

Jay is perhaps best known for his landmark effort against the notorious Hells Angels. He was the first-ever lawman to defeat the gang's multilayered security measures, getting inside to become a member of their legendary Skull Valley charter.

Jay's book about that investigation, *No Angel: My Harrowing Undercover Journey to the Inner Circle of the Hells Angels*, is a *New York Times* and international bestseller. His follow-up book, *Catching Hell: A True Story of Abandonment and Betrayal*, is a memoir that details the events of his life and career.

Jay is a highly sought public speaker, relating his unique experiences to corporate audiences and providing training for 1st Responder events across the country.

JENNIFER FINNIGAN

ACTRESS

I can barely believe it when I say it out loud, but I've been in the entertainment business for over twenty years. And I'm still getting hired, which I guess is a good sign!

I suppose I attribute my success to a few key elements. Obviously, skill is a factor. And luck . . . you need luck in this business. But more than anything, and something I'm very proud of, is the **kindness and professionalism** I've always displayed. Or at least that's always been my intention. I work very hard, I'm not a complainer, and I pride myself on my work ethic.

I'M CONSTANTLY STRIVING TO LEARN MORE, AND I'M NEVER CONTENT TO JUST COAST.

Even as a young actress starting out in my teens, **I would keenly observe what everyone was doing.** Not just the other actors but also the film crew, the ADs, the director, and the producers. I wanted to know *everything* about the business, in front of and behind the cameras, and then apply that knowledge to my work. Being in the know gave me confidence, and with that confidence came greater skill. People took notice. **They knew they could rely on me to deliver.** And slowly but surely, I was given a bigger storyline, an important arc, a producing credit, and more responsibilities—the "heavy lifting," so to speak. And I was scrappy—I still am! **I fought for every job . . . until I didn't have to fight so hard anymore.**

When it felt like I had graduated to a certain level in my acting career, I chose to challenge myself further by codirecting a movie with my husband. Talk about a humbling experience! It felt like starting all over again. I was unsure of every choice, nervous to make mistakes. **That fear made me want to work harder and be better.**

I love what I do. Even after all these years, I'm still passionate about it. It's not an easy life—I'm constantly picking up and moving away from loved ones to film in faraway locations, constantly subject to criticism and self-doubt, and always wondering when the next job will come. It's easy to get swallowed up by fears. But that will get you nowhere. **Be brave. Work hard.**

NEVER STOP LEARNING AND STRIVING TO IMPROVE.

It may not happen overnight. But when it does, when you achieve the success you've been hoping for, you will know you've *earned* it.

And that feels *damn* good.

[

Jennifer has been a presence on TV and film for over twenty years. She has starred on TV series such as CBS's *Salvation*, FX's *Tyrant*, TNT's *Monday Mornings*, Jerry Bruckheimer's *Close to Home*, ABC's *Better with You*, and several other dramas, comedies, and features.

She was the first person to win three consecutive Daytime Emmys for Best Young Actress for her work on *The Bold and the Beautiful*. She is married to actor Jonathan Silverman and is a proud mother to her daughter, Ella Jack.

]

SELF-TRUST

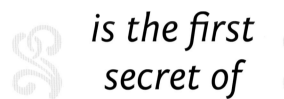

is the first secret of

SUCCESS

Ralph Waldo Emerson

ORONDE GADSDEN

FORMER NFL WIDE RECEIVER FOR THE DALLAS COWBOYS AND MIAMI DOLPHINS

Success to me is making a difference, expanding happiness, living the life you want—not the one you settle for, and reaching worthy goals you set!

5 RULES THAT HELP YOU OBTAIN THAT:

1) Dream big and have a plan.

2) Be persistent.

3) Know what you do, know where to be, and give 100 percent.

4) Power is in the routine.

5) Have a burning desire.

Oronde is a former NFL wide receiver for the Dallas Cowboys and the Miami Dolphins. He devotes a lot of his time to community youth programs and has coordinated and sponsored summer training camps in his hometown of Charleston, South Carolina. He was nominated for ESPY Awards and was the recipient of the AFL Rookie of the Year Honors in 1998, after posting 93 receptions for 1,335 yards, for 38 touchdowns. Mr. Gadsden earned his bachelor of science in business, sports management, and marketing in 1995 on a full four-year scholarship from Winston Salem State.

JESSE ITZLER

ENTREPRENEUR • AUTHOR

like using the **"look at yourself in the mirror"** test as one way to measure success. Ask yourself if you gave all your effort to a task. Ask yourself if you did everything you could to make something work.

REDEFINE SUCCESS AS EFFORT AND NOT THE RESULT.

YOU CAN'T ALWAYS CONTROL THE OUTCOME, BUT YOU CAN ALWAYS CONTROL YOUR EFFORT.

Jesse Itzler only eats fruit until noon, loves Run-DMC, and enjoys living life "out of the box"—actually, he doesn't even have a box. He cofounded Marquis Jet, the world's largest prepaid private jet card company in 2001, which he and his partner sold to Berkshire Hathaway/NetJets in 2009. He then partnered with ZICO Coconut Water, which they sold to the Coca-Cola Company in 2013.

Jesse is a former rapper on MTV, and he produced and sang both the NBA's Emmy Award–winning "I Love This Game" music campaign and the popular New York Knicks anthem "Go NY Go." Itzler is also the author of *Living with a SEAL* (*New York Times* Bestseller, #1 *LA Times*, #1 Amazon, #1 iTunes audiobook) and *Living with the Monks*.

When he's not out training for his next one-hundred-mile run or being a dad, Jesse can be found at the NBA's Atlanta Hawks games, where he is an owner of the team. He is married to SPANX founder Sara Blakely, and the couple and their four children live in Atlanta, Georgia.

DIMITRI JAMES

FOUNDER AND CEO OF SKINN COSMETICS

IF YOU NEVER JUMP, YOU'LL NEVER KNOW WHERE YOU CAN LAND.

My success came from following my passion. I always knew that making people look and feel beautiful inspired me, which led me to my success and accomplishments.

I started my cosmetics company in my garage with $2,500 on a credit card because I could no longer ignore my inner voice that told me I had to do it. From past lessons, I learned that even against all odds, **if I believed in what I was doing, I could never fail.**

WHAT WOULD YOU DO IF YOU KNEW YOU COULDN'T FAIL?

Live your dream, work toward your passion, and give it everything you've got. Support and encourage others to do the same because **nice people do finish first.**

Dimitri James was a beauty industry insider from day one—his mother and *both* grandmothers were European-trained estheticians who made their own skincare products from the finest natural ingredients. It was in this unique environment that Dimitri absorbed the values that drove him to this day: in products, as in people, true beauty isn't about fancy packaging or a slick exterior . . . *What Counts Is Inside.™*

As a licensed esthetician and makeup artist for some of the world's most iconic beauty brands (Estée Lauder, Chanel, Revlon, Lancôme, and Borghese among them) Dimitri dreamed of bringing the luxury skincare experience to a wider audience. In 2002, he realized that dream as the founder of Skinn Cosmetics: high-quality, expertly formulated natural ingredients—in refreshingly no-frills packaging—sold on HSN.

Today, Dimitri is involved in every step of product development, from visiting the organic ingredients to traveling the world exploring the latest beauty trends. His high-energy, informative live makeovers, and genuine love for transforming lives have earned him legions of loyal fans across the globe.

PAT JOHNSON
MARTIAL ARTS CHOREOGRAPHER

My whole life has been a struggle. I quickly learned at a young age that in order to survive—let alone be successful—**I had to be persistent, strong willed, and determined.** I was inspired by my mother, who was abandoned by my father and left to raise eleven children alone. At that time, the law allowed authorities to take children from parents who were not able to provide a normal lifestyle. When I was two, six of us were taken away from my mother and sent to an orphanage in Buffalo, New York. My mother, who had a fourth-grade education, could have given up on us, but instead, she fought to get us back home, even though it took seven years to finally happen. **To this day, she is my fighting inspiration.**

I first met Chuck Norris at a tournament in Detroit shortly after we both served in the military in South Korea, where we learned the martial art Tang Soo Do. Chuck said, "If you should decide to come to California, I think we could work well together." It wasn't long after that I jumped on a Greyhound bus and rode to California. Though the struggles would be many in my career, it was my early experiences and my mother instilling the "never give up" mentality that made me successful as a martial artist and in the film industry.

TO BE SUCCESSFUL, ONE MUST HAVE A GOAL. LET NOTHING DISTRACT YOU OR DISCOURAGE YOU FROM OBTAINING OR REACHING THAT GOAL.

Mr. Johnson is a ninth-degree black belt in the art of American Tang Soo Do and the president of the National Tang Soo Do Congress, which was originally created by Chuck Norris. Pat is known for his martial arts choreography in the *Karate Kid* franchise. He also starred as the All Valley Karate Tournament head referee. Pat Johnson has worked as a choreographer and actor in several films, including *Teenage Mutant Ninja Turtles*, *Mortal Kombat*, and *Enter the Dragon*. He is the recipient of *Black Belt Magazine*'s Instructor of the Year award.

SHAWN JOHNSON

U.S. OLYMPIC GOLD MEDALIST

Success is an elusive goal. I find that once I achieve a certain goal I have set, I often set an even more ambitious target. In my experience, it is important to always set aggressive goals but never put too much pressure on yourself to get there.

WHETHER YOU ARE AIMING FOR A GOLD MEDAL OR A NEW YEAR'S RESOLUTION, BEING SELF-FORGIVING AND DETERMINED AT THE SAME TIME IS KEY.

At twenty-five years old, Shawn Johnson has accomplished a lifetime of achievements that include competing in the Olympics, writing a *New York Times* best-selling book, starting a business, making a career in broadcast, and taking home the coveted Mirrorball trophy on ABC's *Dancing with the Stars*. Hundreds of millions of viewers worldwide watched as a sixteen-year-old Johnson won four medals, including gold on the balance beam, at the 2008 Summer Olympics, which took place in Beijing, China.

Shawn has built a massive digital media presence and has leveraged her platforms to connect with her fans and subscribers that have been with her since she was a young girl. In June 2018, Shawn launched fytlife.com, her lifestyle brand that encompasses apparel, accessories, and health and wellness classes.

SEAN KANAN
ACTOR • PRODUCER • AUTHOR

Much of what I have learned about success has come from my father. He has instilled in me a strong work ethic and an innate sense of civility and kindness to others. I am a firm believer that **very few situations in life represent a binary, zero-sum game, meaning one must lose for another to win.** However, when these times arise, you must act without hesitation—not an easy thing to do, but something winners achieve consistently.

As a young actor, I stood in a line of over fifteen hundred hopefuls, all hoping to win the coveted role of karate's bad boy "Mike Barnes" in *The Karate Kid Part III*. *Rocky* director and Academy Award–winner Jon Avildsen moved through the line, occasionally stopping to speak with an actor. As I saw him making his way toward me, I knew I would have maybe two seconds to catch his attention. With his camera crew in tow, Jon stopped in front of me. He asked me to do a very quick improv of me intimidating him. I must have brought my A game that day. He brought me inside the studio sound stage, where I was immediately placed in an audition scene with the film's star, Ralph Macchio. A very short year before, I had been an audience member in the theater watching *The Karate Kid Part II*. Truly surreal. I went on to win the role, which put me on the map.

SUCCESS MEANS DIFFERENT THINGS AT DIFFERENT TIMES IN OUR LIVES.

I define success less by material accomplishment and largely by the quality of my relationships and my ability to inspire others. **Life has taught me the difference between feeling good and achieving actual happiness.** It is entirely possible to feel temporary emotional or physical discomfort and still be happy. This brilliant life lesson I attribute to my wife, Michele.

Success has common denominators. My acting teacher, the late Roy London, said that he had more in common with a successful plumber than an unsuccessful acting teacher. Successful people largely share specific qualities and employ similar operational tactics and strategies, albeit in very different environments.

I try my best to listen to the knowledge and wisdom of others. My grandpa Sidney, a member of the greatest generation, taught me that advice is free, so listen. If it's valuable, use it, and if not, it has taught you something about the individual offering it.

HERE ARE A FEW PIECES OF ADVICE THAT HAVE HELPED ME:

- **Dream big and dare to fail.** Only by taking risks can success be achieved.

- **Stand on the shoulders of giants.** Follow in the footsteps of others who have achieved what you seek to achieve, but never fear the road less traveled.

- When faced with an overwhelming challenge, heed the words of the Navy SEALs: **"How do you eat a two-thousand-pound elephant? One bite at a time."**

- **Have a plan but remain flexible.** Life is a crafty pitcher capable of throwing fastballs at your head—tricky and unexpected curveballs as well as the occasional screwball, often in the form of a fellow human. Mike Tyson said, "Everyone has a plan until they get punched in the mouth." Always have a contingency.

- Inside each of us rages a personal battle often unbeknownst to those around us. **Seek to win the battle within, and true success will follow.**

- **Last, have fun.**

Sean Kanan epitomizes the expression "triple threat," having achieved success as an actor, a producer, and a writer. He is well known for his breakout performance as the villain Mike Barnes in *The Karate Kid Part III*, where he beat out over fifteen hundred hopefuls; his iconic roles in daytime television playing black sheep AJ Quartermaine on *General Hospital*; and his critically acclaimed portrayal of Deacon Sharpe on *The Bold and the Beautiful*, television's most syndicated show in history, which has been seen in over one hundred countries. Sean has produced five feature films and appeared in over a dozen. He is also the author of *The Modern Gentleman: Cooking and Entertaining with Sean Kanan*.

Sean splits his time between Los Angeles and Palm Springs, and he dedicates his free time to charitable endeavors, practicing martial arts, traveling, and learning multiple foreign languages.

I MEAN TO MAKE MYSELF
A MAN,
AND IF I SUCCEED IN THAT,
I SHALL SUCCEED IN
EVERYTHING ELSE.

James A. Garfield

DON KING

BOXING PROMOTER • PRESIDENT AND CEO OF DON KING PRODUCTIONS

Success as defined by *Merriam-Webster*:

"THE FACT OF GETTING OR ACHIEVING WEALTH, RESPECT, OR FAME."

While defined as a fact, **success truly is a personally and individually subjective word that is viewed differently by every person on the planet.** Some predicate success by the money in their bank accounts, or properties or companies owned, or the names and numbers in their phone or Rolodex, be they celebrities or world leaders. Others view success as having a roof over the heads of their family and food on the table.

As a black man living in America, you must first acknowledge and accept the fact that you are handicapped—by color, Black Codes (unjust laws), customs, and traditions. But I was taught to believe in God, believe in yourself, trust in God, and refuse to accept those handicaps, but never forget that they exist and that they are real. Through my trust in the Lord, I was blessed with self-confidence and a "never say failure" attitude. **I constantly reached for the stars in my every endeavor. I learned that people are my most important asset.** Through self-confidence, giving glory to the Lord for his blessing, it has enabled me to be successful in my efforts to break records and knock down barriers and has empowered me to change hate-filled attitudes with love and a never-fail attitude.

I have totally eliminated the word *failure* from my vocabulary. Setbacks, every now and then . . . **Failure, never.**

I PERSEVERE IN SPITE OF THE ODDS AGAINST ME. NOT BECAUSE OF THE ODDS AGAINST ME.

I never quit because I live in the greatest country in the world based upon America's founding principles: liberty, justice, equality, freedom, and peace. I live, work, believe, and achieve by faith. Predicated on my self-confidence that whatever I undertake to achieve or pursue, I never give up, I never give in, and I never quit. Success is my mission. I live by faith, not by sight. This empowers me to fight for the rights of my fellow man and woman while discussing the plight of my fellow Americans suffering at the hands of a corrupt, rigged, sexist, racist system of governing and control, seeking change . . . Joyfully shaking hands with our president and our elected representatives for the past fifty years working together—**hopefully for a better America.**

Presently, we all individually and collectively need to work together toward achieving success by continuing to break down what divides us—which is a corrupt, rigged, sexist, and racist system. Then, as a nation, we need to **put aside the hatred of our differences** in race, color, religious creed, national origin, or ancestry and **come together as one America** with love, tolerance, understanding, and respect for other people's cultures, with education, acceptance, and wisdom.

THAT TRULY WOULD BE SUCCESS: ONE NATION, UNDER GOD, INDIVISIBLE, WITH LIBERTY, EQUALITY, AND JUSTICE FOR ALL.

One of the most recognizable figures in the world, Don King coined the phrase, "Only in America." The world's greatest promoter lives it. He breathes it. He believes it. A product of the hard-core Cleveland ghetto, he beat the system and made millionaires out of many boxing greats. His shocking hairstyle, infectious smile, booming laugh, and inimitable vocabulary have made Don King universally recognizable. He is known for putting together some of the greatest promotions in boxing history—"The Rumble in the Jungle" and the "Thrilla in Manila"—as well as promoting some of the sport's greatest names in Mike Tyson, George Foreman, Larry Holmes, Joe Frazier, and Julio Cesar Chavez. King has a heart of gold, always donating to those in need. He is truly a champion of the people.

IF YOU WISH IN THIS WORLD TO *advance,*

YOUR MERITS YOU'RE BOUND TO *enhance;*

YOU MUST *stir it* AND *stump it,*

AND *blow your own trumpet,*

OR TRUST ME, YOU HAVEN'T A CHANCE.

W. S. GILBERT

MARTIN KOVE

ACTOR

My fondest memories of great advice came from Sean Connery and James Mason. I was working on the film *Anderson Tapes* as Sean Connery's stand-in, a glorified extra with more luxuries. I had recently been accepted to the NYU School of the Arts for my fifth year at college and at the same time received entrance into the Classic Stage Company (CSC Repertory). I asked Sean, "What should I do? Join a classical repertory company or finish the fifth year at university?"

He quickly responded, **"Young man, if you can do Antigone, you can do anything!"** Obviously, he was suggesting going out there in the world by your bootstraps and trying to make it day by day as an actor looking for work outside of the security of university. I took his advice.

My second adventure with golden advice was meeting James Mason at the airport one day while visiting my parents in New York. I proposed the same question to James Mason as I did to Sean Connery, and he was very kind and offered exactly the same response. He said,

"GO OUT THERE, BOY, AND IF THEY DON'T HIRE YOU, IT'S THEIR MISTAKE. YOU MUST LOOK AT THE GAMBLE OF YOUR LIFE WITH THAT PERSPECTIVE."

I have often given that advice to young actors who come up and ask, "What's the best advice you can give me, and what do you think your break was?" **I don't think I've had my break yet, which keeps me driven to compete and establish myself with only good work.** And I believe if you seek to establish yourself as a fine actor with the creation of only good work that's meaningful to your heart and career, then you could never lead yourself astray more than being in the company of those who have become actors for the sole purpose of becoming famous and rich.

Martin Kove was born in Brooklyn, New York, and was raised with a Jewish upbringing. He has appeared in over eighty feature films and television shows, including *Rambo: First Blood Part II* and *Cagney & Lacey*. His most notable role has been the iconic Sensei John Kreese in *The Karate Kid* (1984), *The Karate Kid Part II* (1986), and *The Karate Kid Part III* (1989). He is currently reprising his role in the wildly successful spinoff *Cobra Kai*, seen on YouTube Premium. He has black belts in the martial arts Kendo, Okinawa-te, and Tiger Kenpo.

DON'T FEAR FAILURE.
NOT FAILURE, BUT LOW AIM, IS THE CRIME.

IN GREAT ATTEMPTS IT IS *glorious* EVEN TO FAIL.

BRUCE LEE

MIKE KRZYZEWSKI

HEAD MEN'S BASKETBALL COACH
AT DUKE UNIVERSITY

M y mom never went to high school. And she said to me, "Mike, get on the right bus. You are going to start driving your own bus now, and it's going to take you through different neighborhoods. **Only let good people on it, and only get on other good people's buses.**"

She said, and it was so prophetic,

"YOUR BUS WILL GO TO PLACES THAT YOU COULD NEVER GO ALONE."

Now in his thirty-ninth season at Duke, Mike Krzyzewski—a Naismith Hall of Fame coach, five-time national champion, and twelve-time Final Four participant—has built a dynasty that few programs in the history of the game can match.

The numbers that illustrate Coach K's career are staggering, including 5 national championships, 6 gold medals as head coach of the US Men's National Team, 1,045 victories at Duke (the most in NCAA history at one school), and 1,118 career wins (the most in NCAA history).

Coach K has led the Blue Devils into the NCAA Tournament thirty-four times—more than any other coach in NCAA history. He has taken Duke to the NCAA Tournament in each of the last twenty-three seasons, the longest active streak by a coach and tied for the longest in NCAA history.

JILL LIBERMAN

MOTIVATIONAL SPEAKER • AUTHOR

Success begins with a dream, so my first piece of advice for achieving success is dream big! After you know what you want, you need to take action. Just go for it! Nothing is going to happen until you make it happen. Mark Twain said,

"THE SECRET OF GETTING AHEAD IS GETTING STARTED."

Be grateful for everything, even the bumps along the way. Attitude and a positive mindset are so important. As a motivational speaker and founder of Choose Happy, I give talks all over the world about the power of happiness. I believe that when you are happy, anything is possible. Success and happiness are not interchangeable.

HAPPINESS CAN BRING SUCCESS, BUT SUCCESS BY ITSELF DOES NOT EQUAL HAPPINESS.

The secret to success is knowing what you want, believing it is possible, developing a plan to help you see it through, and staying committed. **Turning your dreams into reality requires time and effort, so be patient!** Success results from practice, determination, sacrifice, focus, and commitment. Have fun on your journey. Own it. As demonstrated by the stories and advice shared in this book, anything is possible.

THE TIME IS NOW. GO CREATE YOUR MASTERPIECE!

Jill Liberman is a sought-after motivational speaker and published author with more than twenty years of experience in the media and television industries. Jill was an active member of NATPE, the National Association of Television Program Executives, and a judge for the nationally televised Cable Ace awards. She has been chairperson and judge for the international Stevie Awards for the last five years recognizing women in business. Jill hosted the number-one rated talk show on WAXY radio and cohosted the television pilot "Thicke and Jill" with actor Alan Thicke.

American Pride, Jill's first book and a stirring tribute to America, received national recognition on television shows, radio, and magazines. The White House had a copy of her book displayed in the lobby, and her story was featured on television as one of the most inspirational women in America. Jill has been featured in numerous publications, including *USA Today* and *Success Magazine*. She graduated from George Washington University with a degree in psychology. *Success Factor X* is Ms. Liberman's fourth book.

Somebody said **IT COULDN'T BE DONE,**

But he with a chuckle replied

That "maybe it couldn't," but he would be one

Who wouldn't say so till he'd tried.

So he buckled right in with the trace of a grin

On his face. If he worried he hid it.

He started to sing as he tackled the thing

That couldn't be done, **AND HE DID IT.**

—Edgar A. Guest

KATE LINDER

ACTRESS

To achieve success, you must never give up. Do what you can to the very best of your ability and don't look for the end result. It is called show business because it is the business of show and performing, and you must treat it as such. Acting is a craft, and to this day, I continue to go to my acting classes and to my voice and dance lessons.

NEVER BE COMPLACENT; THERE IS ALWAYS MORE TO LEARN.

As with any creative endeavor, try to practice daily. When you encounter rejection (and everybody does) ask for feedback and **consider this constructive criticism as another opportunity for growth.** How fortunate I am to be able to continue working at what I love to do. I will never give up and will always remain focused and grateful.

Kate Linder has portrayed Esther Valentine on CBS's *The Young and the Restless*, the number-one-rated (for thirty years!) soap opera, for thirty-six years. In 2008, Linder received a star on the Hollywood Walk of Fame. Linder has a busy feature film career as well. She has starred in the recent feature films *Hysteria*, *Erased*, *Miss Meadows*, Garry Marshall's *Mother's Day* and *The Charnel House*, and Charlie Matthau's *Book of Leah*, *Stereotypically You*, *Voice from the Stone*, and *Dead Love*.

Linder has been the celebrity spokesperson for the ALS Association for over a decade since her late brother-in-law's initial diagnosis. She has lobbied Congress on their behalf and won several of their volunteer awards for her efforts. Linder also is a longtime board member for SAG-AFTRA and a former two-time governor of the Television Academy. She is active with countless charities that benefit research and support for health-related causes, and she hosts three annual charity teas in Canada that benefit the March of Dimes (Canada's Conductive Education program) and Canucks for Kids. Linder also works with the Los Angeles Mission and makes trips visiting troops with the USO.

DR. SHICA LITTLE
CREATOR OF INCREDIWHIP

Before my father passed away, I recall him being adamant in wanting me to take care of the family and to be a success. **I worked especially hard to achieve the most I could in order to fulfill my dad's dying wish.** After the passing of my dad, I spent a lot of time with my grandmother while my mother worked. I often watched my grandmother in the kitchen studying her recipe books. She encouraged me to be creative in the kitchen. Later in life I decided to make a lifestyle change that included making better food choices. I'm a southern girl who likes to splurge sometimes. Unfortunately, most of my guilty pleasures were made with high-fructose corn syrup or artificial flavors and colors. Like my grandma always said,

"IF YOU CAN'T FIND SOMETHING, CREATE IT!"

Her advice inspired me to create IncrediWhip.

MY ADVICE FOR OTHERS WHO WANT TO ACHIEVE SUCCESS IS "DON'T BE AFRAID TO ACT."

Planning is critical, but at some point, you have to take the facts gathered and act on them.

Dr. Shica came up with the idea for creating her product while completing her doctoral degree and teaching college at Grand Canyon University. After teaching classes, she would come home and work on her dissertation, often drinking several cups of coffee to help her stay awake. As an avid coffee drinker, Dr. Shica came to realize that all the stuff she was putting in her coffee was not healthy. She became determined not to cream her coffee with artificial ingredients, which began her quest to create better-for-you food products. After many failed attempts, she finally came up with a winning recipe that immediately gained the interest of retail buyers. With the successful launch of her line of whipped cream behind her, she began development on her latest idea: a unique blend of natural flavors, colors, and sweeteners that are premeasured in ready-to-use packs.

BEN LIVELY

PROFESSIONAL BASEBALL PITCHER, KANSAS CITY ROYALS

Success means to me that you're willing to do *anything* to make sure that your goal is accomplished—whatever it takes. As Ernest Hemingway said,

"MAN IS NOT MADE FOR DEFEAT. A MAN CAN BE DESTROYED BUT NOT DEFEATED."

Ben Lively is a professional baseball pitcher for the Kansas City Royals. He made his Major League debut in 2017. After his first career homer, he became the first Phillies pitcher to homer since 2015, and when he homered again, he became the first Philadelphia pitcher to homer twice in a season since 2011. Before playing in the MLB, Ben received the Paul Owens Award as the top pitcher in the Phillies minor league system. He was named a Pioneer League All-Star in his first professional season. Ben was also named a top-ten prospect in the Reds' minor league system by *Baseball America*. In high school, he lettered in baseball, football, and basketball, and then he went on to attend the University of Central Florida (UCF).

SUSAN LUCCI

ACTRESS

S tudying in college, I was lucky enough to have a professor that once impressed upon all of his students that pursing acting could be a devastating career choice. He explained that rejection can be demoralizing, as can the work. He said, "If acting is making you miserable as human beings, then the pursuit is not worth it. And, if you are one of the lucky few who do make it out there, don't go into a bubble. **Don't allow yourself to become so out of touch or removed from humanity that you can no longer experience and express humanity.**" I have never forgotten those poignant and impactful words.

THE BEAUTY IN THE WORD *SUCCESS* IS THAT IT REMAINS SUBJECTIVE.

Each one of us has a beautiful interpretation of such a dynamic word. I am so grateful to all of my teachers both on and off the screen who have taught me that following your dreams, no matter how big they are, leads to inevitable happiness. I was once told that human beings need four things in life to be happy: **response, recognition, security, and adventure.** Finding the balance of these four things is a measure of success.

I strived to live my life to honor these lessons I was lucky enough to receive. Along the way, however, I have learned that the greatest inspiration in life, and what has ultimately led to my "success," is the greatest gift of all—love. To me, if you have love in your life, you love someone who loves you back. **And if you can do what you love and love what you do, you have found the true meaning of success.**

IT ALL BEGINS WITH A DREAM.

The reigning queen of daytime television, Susan Lucci held audiences spellbound for nearly five decades as the famed and fiery Erica Kane on ABC's *All My Children*. With more than twenty Emmy nominations, Susan made television history in 1999 when she finally won the Emmy Award for "Best Actress," becoming the most-nominated actor in television history. Her iconic career led her to roles in the primetime drama *Devious Maids*, her part in the highly acclaimed movie *Joy*, and her Broadway debut as Annie Oakley in *Annie Get Your Gun*. Susan earned her star on the Hollywood Walk of Fame in 2005. She was inducted into the Broadcasting Hall of Fame in 2006 and released her *New York Times* best-selling autobiography, *All My Life*, in 2011.

I'm a *success*
today because
I had a *friend*
who believed in me,
and I didn't have
the *heart*
to let him down.

Abraham Lincoln

DARRYL MCDANIELS

FOUNDING MEMBER OF RUN-DMC

MY THOUGHTS ON SUCCESS: D-M-C.
DETERMINATION — MOTIVATION — COMMITMENT.

don't think success can only be defined in terms of accomplishments and goals achieved. **Failures are successful ventures, or should I say adventures.** Because when you fail at something, you come out of that experience learning something. It's all about the experience and the lesson!

Experiences, whether good or bad, allow you to learn. And that's a good thing! You learn about yourself, you learn about others, and you learn about the thing(s) you are trying to do. The experience creates knowledge, and knowledge creates wisdom. But it's not over because now you know there's more you can do! It's all in the doing!

It's about doing things and loving and enjoying what you are doing despite the outcome. I've done many things and failed but had a hell of a good time doing them.

SUCCESS IS NOT JUST DEFINITIVE POSITION.

For example, I can't just "be" a great professional basketball player, but I can get out there and play basketball and learn in the process what it would take to be a great professional basketball player and in turn understand what I can and cannot do. So . . . I realize or learn I really can't be on the San Antonio Spurs! And that's not a bad thing! It's *good* because now I know; I can't get out there and battle Lebron, Curry, and Westbrook—but I can go play any time I want and have fun doing it!

We can't literally "be" everything we want to be, but we can DO whatever we want to do, and regardless of the outcome, that will lead you to "experiences" (successes) beyond your wildest dreams! In your doing, for that time you are doing it, you are!

For me, I loved rock music! I loved hip hop! I was writing rhymes and deejaying because it was fun. I didn't start out wanting to BE a businessman or BE famous or BE a rock star or BE a rapper.

I didn't even really want to be in the "music business," but just by me doing (because it was fun and made me feel good) what John Lennon, Mick Jagger, Harry Chapin, Grandmaster Caz, and Grandmaster Flash were doing . . . I became all of those things. But my worldwide historical "success" cannot be compared to many others you may not even know about! Am I *more* successful than the teacher who has impacted the lives of students for many, many decades? Am I more successful than the individual who lived the most messed-up life of drugs and despair but now shares their experience with people to inspire, save, and change the lives of others? A big, thick, loud, noisy, hard-hitting NO! **These individuals may never be rich or famous, so even though I'm "known," it cannot be said I'm more successful than them!**

See, it's all about the experiences. What have you done? What are you doing? What are you going to do or want to do? Do you have good intentions, and do you want to do good things and bring good to others?

If so, that's when the magic happens. **Go do it! Try to do it! Have fun!** Some good will come out of it. Remember the song, "Do whatcha want to, do it everyone. Do what you want to, just have some fun!"

You may not be King James like Lebron! But there are sooo many things you can DO to BE in the NBA and have a so-called "successful" career in the NBA. Be a sportscaster on radio or TV, a trainer, a doctor, lawyer, agent, manager, etc.

All those things are possible! You may not be King DMC, but I can't achieve without a team of folks DOING things for me to DO what I need to DO to BE who I am: lights, sound, publicist, manager, agents, accountants, and lawyers. All of these things allow people to have a "successful" career in music. **The most successful person in the world is the person getting up every day with good intentions, doing what makes them happy, regardless of the outcome!** Just because no one is filming or blogging about them doesn't mean they're not successful.

SUCCESS IS THE SPREADING AND SHARING OF GOODNESS, KINDNESS, TRUTH, RESPECT, AND LOVE.

Now don't get me wrong, having a goal and achieving the desired outcome can be a form of success. But legitimate success can only be through hard work, dedication, determination, (good) motivation, commitment, and concentration! I say all of this to ask this final question to all of you: Do you consider the person who lied, cheated, stole, killed, and destroyed lives to obtain wealth, power, or notoriety a success? **How you answer that question will determine if you really know what success is!**

Darryl "DMC" McDaniels is cofounder of the legendary group Run-DMC, which has sold over forty million albums and changed music history.

In 2014, he started his comic book company, Darryl Makes Comics. In 2016, he released the top-selling autobiography *Ten Ways Not to Commit Suicide*. And in November 2017, he put out a limited-edition vinyl EP in advance of his upcoming solo album.

In 2006, DMC cofounded the Felix Organization—a nonprofit that works to enrich the lives of children in the foster care system. He's a 2009 Rock & Roll Hall of Fame inductee, a 2016 Grammy Lifetime Achievement Award recipient, and an award-winning philanthropist.

PRINCE LORENZO DE' MEDICI

PHILANTHROPIST • HEIR TO THE MEDICI DYNASTY

As Prince Lorenzo de' Medici, I live by the motto which my family has utilized for generations since the time of my ancestor Lorenzo il Magnifico. **That motto is *Sempre*.** In the Italian language, *sempre* means "always"—always faithful to the community, always faithful to the business, and, of course, always faithful to the family. These were the main rules of success for the Medici family from years gone by until today.

The Medici family were the most important family in banking during Renaissance Italy. In fact, we invented the use of checks that previously did not exist. They were called a promise of payment. **Appearing in our family crest are the words *love, hope*, and *charity*.** These, too, are fundamental concepts for success. In my case, venture capitalism and philanthropy are in my DNA. For me, this means giving back to others through our company. This is what has created my success.

We have an old saying in my family which loosely translates to

"WORK HARD AND HAVE FUN, BECAUSE THE FUTURE IS UNKNOWN."

Enjoy the work you do and live in the present with an eye toward the future and constant innovation. This is important for me both as an artist and as a businessman.

Equally as important is the relationship we have with failure, which can be a great teacher. The master Leonardo da Vinci originally opened a restaurant that did not succeed. He came to the Medici and was hired as a wedding planner and decorator. During a royal wedding, the food arrived cold to the royal. From this, da Vinci built a precursor to the microwave oven. **The lesson from this story is that from failure often arises success.** It is also very important to align yourself with talented individuals who may be smarter or more talented than you. These are my secrets to success and prosperity.

Prince Lorenzo de' Medici is a Renaissance man in the truest sense of the expression. His father is a direct descendant from the historic Florentine family, and his mother descends from Polish princes. The Medici family have always been philanthropists and patrons of the arts and sciences. Prince Lorenzo is a gifted artist in his own right and continues his family's tradition of philanthropy and service. He lives by the personal motto, "Let's make the nobility a useful service to the less fortunate."

Prince Lorenzo resides in Los Angeles and Rome, the eternal city, with his wife, Rosemary, and daughter, Maddalena.

THERE IS ONLY ONE SUCCESS...

TO BE ABLE TO SPEND YOUR LIFE IN YOUR OWN WAY, AND NOT TO GIVE OTHERS ABSURD MADDENING CLAIMS UPON IT.

CHRISTOPHER MORLEY

ANDREW NEIDERMAN

AUTHOR • GHOSTWRITER • PRODUCER

SUCCESS IS OFTEN MISTAKEN FOR MONETARY GAIN. TRUE SUCCESS IS SOMETHING NO ONE BUT YOU CAN SEE AND FEEL.

I was fortunate to begin my professional career as a teacher. Perhaps no other profession is clearly measured not by money but by the self-satisfaction one senses when he or she can see precisely how his or her words and actions affected younger people.

My second career, my lifelong desire, was as a writer. And while it is true that well-known authors today are people who earn great wealth as well as fame, the satisfaction truly lies in the work you've created, how true to life it is, and how well it will please and move your readers so that when they are finished reading one of your works, they feel they have been somewhere else and known so many other people, the people you created.

A second satisfaction comes from the pleasure you see in your family when they share in your accolades. I was honored often in my life, but one time when I was the honorary for the Act for MS charity, garnering one of their largest crowds at their gala, I recall thinking that **the only great value to fame is how you can use it to help others.**

Beyond that, it is really only a fifteen-minute glory, and when that's over, **if that's all you wanted, you are not successful.** You are someone to pity. You missed the whole point of your own life.

SUCCESS SIMPLY MEANS THE TAKING OF JOY FROM THE ONES YOU HAVE HELPED ACHIEVE SUCCESS OF THEIR OWN AND FROM THE LOVE YOUR FAMILY HAS FOR WHAT YOU HAVE DONE AND WHO YOU HAVE BEEN.

Along with his own forty-six publications, the most famous of which is *The Devil's Advocate*, Andrew Neiderman has published over 125 novels, ten of which have been adapted into films. He has coauthored the screenplay for *Duplicates* and written the screenplay for V. C. Andrews's *RAIN*, which featured Academy Award–winner Faye Dunaway and nominee Robert Loggia. Andrew Neiderman has cowritten the libretto for the stage musical of *The Devil's Advocate*, set to premiere in South Korea. The stage play of *The Devil's Advocate* will be on a UK tour in the fall of 2019.

Since Neiderman began his V. C. Andrews authorship, the franchise has gone from just under 30 million books worldwide to now just over 107 million, making Neiderman the most successful ghostwriter in literary history. V. C. Andrews has been published independently in ninety-five countries and translated into twenty-six languages. The international scope of the franchise continues this day with publications through the United Kingdom, Holland, Germany, and now Mainland China. Under his coproducing activities, he has helped successfully place ten V. C. Andrews titles on Lifetime and is heavily involved in a television series development of the entire *Flowers in the Attic* series for Lifetime.

Andrew Neiderman often speaks to international and domestic audiences interested in publishing and film.

It had long since come
to my attention that

PEOPLE OF ACCOMPLISHMENT

rarely sat back and let things
happen to them.

They went out and

HAPPENED TO THINGS.

∘ Leonardo da Vinci ∘

JON PRITIKIN

INSPIRATIONAL SPEAKER •
COFOUNDER OF FEEL THE POWER

Over the last two decades of circling the world, I have come to learn some secrets that have made me who and what I am today.

ONE: ALWAYS PURSUE RELATIONSHIPS AND NOT CONNECTIONS.

Relationships will last not just for your career but also for your life. The connections or working engagements you strive for will come out of the friendship you build. Never let it be the driving force. Just enjoy the friendship.

TWO: BE KIND.

While an easy statement in actuality, it is a difficult one to live out. Life is challenging enough. **Trying to just be nice throughout those trials can be hard to navigate.** However, just by being nice you will see your journey and the lives of those around you forever changed.

THREE: BE REAL.

That seems obvious but it's actually difficult. With social media, TV, and movies always saying we should be one thing, being yourself can actually be hard. My friend once said, **"You are born an original. Don't die as a copy."** Learning to be me and not trying to be something else has opened doors and sky-rocketed my career.

My life ambition is to help students know how special they are. Growing up with some speech and learning disabilities made my social life difficult to say the least. But having the internal drive to never give up is something I always want my audience to know. **Tough times come, but they don't last forever.** I might not be the best communicator, but I want to be the best connector. If I do that, every attendee will walk out knowing how truly special they are.

For over two decades, Jon Pritikin has traveled the world motivating and inspiring people of all ages by using feats of strength as a platform to share his "never give up" story. Outside of London, England, on July 11, 2007, Jon broke and set two world records for rolling up frying pans with his bare hands, earning a spot in the *Guinness World Records 2009* book. In 1994, he and his wife, Rhonda, cofounded Feel the Power, a nonprofit anti-bullying school assembly program that has motivated students around the planet.

Having overcome a multitude of obstacles and disabilities and proving wrong all those who spoke the words "You can't," Jon has a gift for speaking to issues of self-worth and to the value of each individual. Whether speaking in school assemblies, with professional athletes, or in the corporate world, Jon uses humor, inspirational narrative, and passion to equip people with the keys to make positive decisions and to help them recognize their true potential. Over eight million people in fifty countries around the world have heard this motivational message.

If you hear a voice within you saying, "You are not a painter," then by all means

Paint...

and that voice will be silenced.

Vincent van Gogh

FORBES RILEY

ACTRESS • BROADCAST JOURNALIST • SUCCESS/RESULTS COACH

Growing up on Long Island, I had a bad overbite and was subjected to full silver railroad braces for eight years (yes, from age eight to sixteen). I had an odd, crooked nose from a misencounter with a baseball bat; my hair was beyond frizzy; and thanks to the dawn of fast food and frozen TV dinners, I was about forty pounds overweight.

By the time I got to college, the nose had been fixed, the braces had been removed, and I had learned to blow-dry my hair "Marcia Brady" straight—but I still battled with the weight. No, actually I battled with the stigma of being an "ugly girl with no talent and a big butt," a phrase from one of the kids who bullied me that always resonated in my brain. My self-image was negative even though I had a burning desire and dream of being on stage as an actress, and often **I would sabotage myself before I even had the chance to fail the audition.**

BUT ONE DAY, SOMETHING CHANGED.

During my senior year in college, the production was Shakespeare's *As You Like It*, and the lead role of Rosalind was one of the greatest written. She's on stage for the better part of two and a half hours, meddling in everyone's life, pretending to be a boy, falling in love, frolicking through a forest, exploring life, and making people laugh. A dream role. I auditioned as I always had in high school, just hoping to land the small role of a townsperson or court jester . . . but lo and behold! When I saw the audition casting sheet, my name was on top for the very first time. What? So I headed to ask Professor Richman, **"Why me? Why now?"** I was graduating to be a lawyer and had already dashed those dreams of being a Broadway actress.

He sat me down and said,

"You have a rare gift of comic timing and insight. The pains you suffered growing up have given you a depth beyond your years. And your voice is deep and full as though you have something to say worth listening to. *You* are my dream Rosalind."

Now notice he didn't comment on the texture of my hair, the bright smile the braces revealed when they were finally removed, or even the extra pounds that gave me a "zaftig" outline in jeans . . . because he never *saw* any one of those superficial features. **Professor David Richman was 100 percent legally blind and the first man to ever really see me.**

For his mentorship and his rock-solid faith and belief in the me I always knew I could be—I owe him. He taught me that **success is how you define it**, that it lives deep inside of you and is something *no one* can take away . . . unless you let them. **So don't let them.**

MY MOTTO TO THIS DAY IS "DREAM IT, BELIEVE IT, ACHIEVE IT." IT REALLY WORKS.

Forbes is one of the world's leading health and wellness experts and a National Fitness Hall of Fame inductee. She was voted the "Top 20 Most Inspiring People on Television" through her roles as a sought-after spokesperson, broadcast journalist, and success/results coach to celebrities, sales teams, and CEOs.

Her career includes a plethora of acting and hosting credits on Broadway, TV series, and movies. She has received best TV presenter awards and hosted numerous infomercials. Forbes launched Forbes Factor LIVE and The Billionaire Business Academy to inspire others.

Forbes has extensive experience in front of and behind the camera working on direct and traditional marketing campaigns.

SUCCESS

is liking yourself,
liking what you do,
and liking

HOW YOU DO IT.

Maya Angelou

TONY ROBBINS

GLOBAL ENTREPRENEUR • SPORTS TEAM OWNER • BUSINESS STRATEGIST

The number-one characteristic of successful people is HUNGER. An insatiable desire to BE more, DO more, CREATE more, and GIVE more.

Successful people do what others won't as a result of their standards. They demand more from themselves than anyone else could ever expect.

I DEFINE SUCCESS AS THE MASTERY OF TWO AREAS:

1) **The Science of Achievement**, or the ability to turn any dream into reality, to produce any result.

2) **The Art of Fulfillment**, or the art of finding joy in the process of whatever life brings; the power to understand, appreciate, and enjoy our lives at the deepest level.

Tony Robbins is the nation's number-one life and business strategist. He is the author of six internationally bestselling books, including the recent *New York Times* number-one bestseller *MONEY: Master the Game* and *UNSHAKEABLE*. He created the number-one personal and professional development program of all time.

Mr. Robbins is the chairman of a holding company composed of forty privately held businesses with combined sales exceeding $5 billion a year. He has been honored by Accenture as one of the "Top 50 Business Intellectuals in the World," by Harvard Business Press as one of the "Top 200 Business Gurus," and by American Express as one of the "Top Six Business Leaders in the World" to coach its entrepreneurial clients. *Fortune*'s recent cover article named him the "CEO Whisperer," and he has been named in the top fifty of *Worth Magazine*'s "100 Most Powerful Men and Women in Global Finance" for three consecutive years.

As a philanthropist, through his partnership with Feeding America, Mr. Robbins has provided over four hundred million meals in the last three years to those in need.

ERIC ROBERTS

ACTOR

THERE IS NO KEY TO SUCCESS. THERE IS A KEY RING TO SUCCESS, WITH INFINITE KEYS ON IT.

Recognize your community's potential. And in that recognition, realize that you will likely work tomorrow "for" those who work "for" you today. **Embrace that.** Shakespeare had it right. **There are tragedies and there are comedies—all part of life.** Embrace what you might want to eliminate. The rough stuff can be your best friend as an artist and throughout your personal character.

Eric Roberts is an Academy Award nominee for his role in *Runaway Train* and a three-time Golden Globe nominee for *Runaway Train*, *Star 80*, and *King of the Gypsies*. He received acclaim at the Sundance Film Festival for his role in *A Guide to Recognizing Your Saints* and *It's My Party*. He also starred in *La Cucaracha*, which won Best Film at the Austin Film Festival, and for which Roberts won Best Actor at the New York Independent Film Festival that same year. Other notable performances include his roles in *The Dark Knight*, *Final Analysis*, *Inherent Vice* for Warner Bros., Millennium Films's *Lovelace*, and *The Expendables* for Lionsgate.

On television, Roberts's memorable recurring roles include characters in USA's *Suits*, CBS's *CSI* and *Code Black*, NBC's *Heroes*, and Starz's *Crash*. He has appeared as a guest star in *Grey's Anatomy*, *Will & Grace*, *Brooklyn Nine-Nine*, *Hawaii Five-O*, *Entourage*, and more.

Upcoming, Roberts plays Matt Dillon's doctor in *Head Full of Honey*, a Warner Bros. Germany production. He also has a supporting role in the independent *Hard Luck Love Song*. He is set to recur as DEA boss "Erick Sheldon" in *La Reina del Sur* for Telemundo Global Studio and Netflix.

Roberts began his career in theatre in New York City, where he won the Theatre World Award for his role on Broadway in *Burn This*. He currently resides in Los Angeles with his wife of twenty-six years and his feline animals.

EDIE RODRIGUEZ

AMERICAS BRAND CHAIRPERSON
FOR PONANT CRUISES

Success is an interesting word. Like beauty, to me it is in the eye of the beholder. It is a very personal and individualized concept. To achieve success, I was told as a child to **get a great education, find my passion, and follow it**. It was great advice that has carried me through my whole life—and continues to carry me forward even today. In the same way that life evolves, my passions are always evolving.

In these times, some see the fact that I was a female CEO and president, and now a chairman, as success. While on some level that is perhaps success by most standards, I never equate a title and successfully delivering ROI as my own version of success for myself. Those things are perhaps important, but to me, they are simply a part of success. I look at success for myself as loving what I am doing, being healthy and happy, having an "attitude of gratitude," having time for my loved ones to create new memories together, and giving back in many different ways, with all of these things concurrently working together.

FOR ME, SUCCESS IS SIMPLY TRULY BEING PASSIONATE ABOUT WHAT I'M DOING IN EVERY ASPECT OF MY LIFE.

It is not defined by a title or by how much income I am earning. If I do not feel passionate about what I'm doing, then that is my own barometer to tell myself it is time for me to do something else and to challenge myself further and create new goals. **I love my life and live it in a perpetual state of evolution and learning and growing.** This is success to me and what excites me. While I have achieved my business goals in life to date, I am consistently creating new goals for myself, so there are so many more successes yet to come. As I look back and forward, success to me means simply loving what I'm doing in this perpetual process.

My advice to anyone seeking success in business and life is to set your goals based on what you are truly passionate about and want to do and then go out each and every day working hard and staying focused on those goals. **Trust your own instincts, not those of your naysayers.** Hard work always pays off, one way or another. Give back every step of the way as well by mentoring someone, giving your time to a favorite charity, helping your community, putting your iPhone down to look your child in the eye during conversation, etc. Giving back does not just have to be in a financial manner either, especially if you are just starting out building your career, since you may not have those means yet.

I have a lot of mini mantras for myself that I call "Edie-isms." One "Edie-ism" is that **"it is better to dare to fail than to fail to dare."** Even if your hard work didn't achieve one of your goals, it should not be looked at as "failure." Those "lessons," not "failures," will typically end up being blessings in disguise and will lead you to perhaps another and even better path.

Oh, and by the way, do not procrastinate. **There is no time like the present, so go now and get started before your competition does.** Write down your own plan for success right now and begin!

I WISH YOU ALL THE SUCCESS IN THE WORLD. HERE'S TO YOUR SUCCESS!

Edie Rodriguez is the Americas Brand chairman and special corporate advisor for Ponant, the world's leading luxury yacht expedition cruise line. Rodriguez has over thirty years of experience in executive roles in the cruise and travel industry and previously served as the CEO and president of Crystal Cruises, where she led the brand's transformation during her tenure. She has also held leadership positions with brands from Carnival Corporation and RCCL Corporation.

Rodriguez is actively involved in the travel industry. She serves on *Robb Report*'s private aviation board and Atout France's advisory board for French tourism, and she was previously on the board of directors for Cruise Line International Association (CLIA) and is a past member of the Promotion Marketing Association. She and Ponant are also strong supporters of Tourism Cares. Rodriguez is a strong voice and advocate in the luxury travel space and has harnessed the power of social media and digital platforms to reach a global audience.

In recognition of her business leadership, she was named Ernst & Young's "Entrepreneur of the Year" in May 2017 and was selected as *Luxury Daily*'s "25 Luxury Women to Watch for 2017." Rodriguez was also named a "Wave Maker" by *Afar*, as one of ten visionaries making travel better in 2016, and was selected as one of the ten most influential people in travel by the editors of Travelpulse.com. She was also named a "Woman of Note" by *The Wall Street Journal* in 2014.

To *travel hopefully*
is a better thing
than to *arrive,*

and the *true success*
is to *labour*.

Robert Louis Stevenson

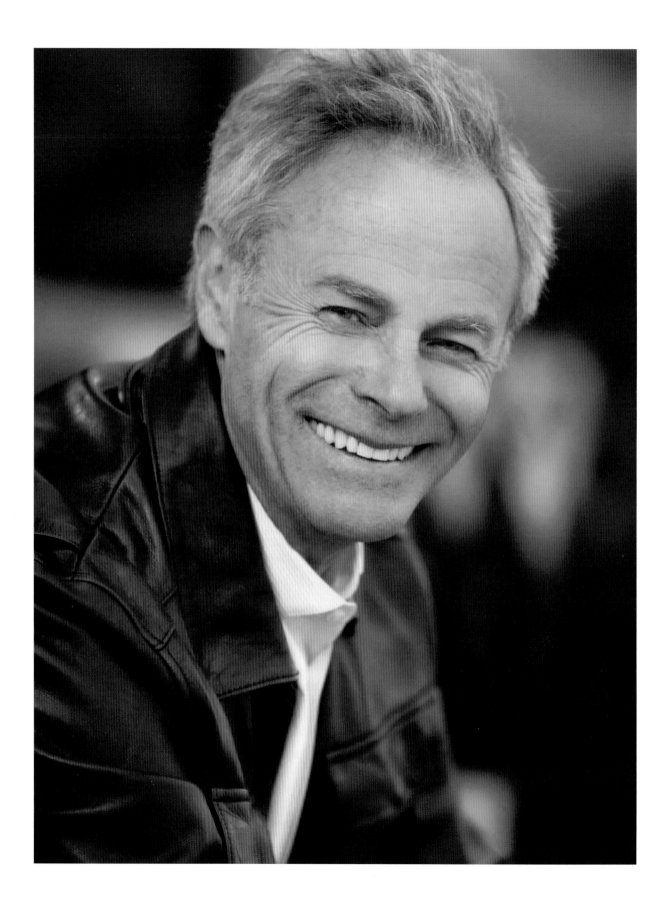

TRISTAN ROGERS

ACTOR

don't have any word, phrase, or rule I worked by to get me where I am. I stumbled for years and was never sure if I was on the right path. When I started to develop commitment to what I was doing, things changed. And this happens a lot. When I went through this transition, the business was different. Today, it appears you make the transition much earlier. But your lifespan in this industry seems to be shorter. The one thing I can convey is **if you have the drive, *you never give up.***

EVEN IF IT LOOKS HOPELESS, JUST STICK IN THERE. YOU NEVER KNOW WHAT'S AROUND THE NEXT CORNER.

And remember to be flexible because with today there are so many options out there. With the options comes a necessity to be able to roll with the punches because your career goes through lots of transitions and changes. Stay true to you and if you're lucky, you'll find a partner who has a like mind and wants to become part of your quest. This is important because it becomes tough doing it by yourself.

And the most important thing I can impart: Develop a thick skin. Rejection in this industry is built in. Most of it isn't personal, but it can be. You rise up and go on to the next interview. And there will always be another. Learn the art of following your path but surviving at the same time. **And that's where a partner is important.** I married someone exceptional. I was lucky—finding that person is tough, and they aren't always obvious. It can take some time.

GOOD LUCK, AND REMEMBER . . . *NEVER GIVE UP.*

Tristan Rogers came to the United States from Australia in 1979 not knowing what the future would hold. In a short period of time, his life was to change forever. He has enjoyed a long and successful acting career as Robert Scorpio on the ABC soap opera *General Hospital*. He was the voice of Jake in Walt Disney Pictures' *The Rescuers Down Under* and starred as Colin Atkinson on the CBS soap opera *The Young and the Restless*.

MIKE ROSEN

RADIO TALK SHOW HOST

LEFT RIGHT LEFT

n these days of our great public divide, your first reaction to this title would likely assume that the reference is to irreconcilable differences between liberals and conservatives. Not the case. Instead, **think of soldiers marching in cadence.** The story begins in Fort Gordon, Georgia. In 1965, at the age of twenty, I had dropped out of college and was quickly scooped up in the Vietnam War military draft. I was soon a US Army buck private stationed at Fort Gordon for basic combat training. It was hot and humid and physically demanding—something of an ordeal, but tolerable and necessary. Our drill instructor, Sergeant First Class Gambrell, wasn't exactly an R. Lee Ermey stereotype (the actor who played the iconic Marine DI Gunnery Sergeant Hartman in the movie *Full Metal Jacket*). Sgt. Gambrell was tough but fair. **He thought I had some leadership qualities and made me a squad leader.**

As a relevant backstory, this took place during a huge national military buildup. Fort Gordon was overwhelmed with new recruits and actually ran out of barracks to house them in. So, my basic training platoon was quartered in six-man canvas tents in a field behind the company area. In the late fall, it got kind of cold at night, and the pot-bellied stoves hadn't arrived to heat the tents. The thin Army blankets weren't up to the job, and just about everybody in our platoon came down with pneumonia. I avoided sick call as long as I could, but I finally succumbed and was sent to the post hospital along with my band of brothers.

Now, the worst thing that can happen to you in basic training is the dreaded "recycle." That's when you're forced to start all over from week one, and it happens if you miss two weeks of training. I was desperate to get out of the hospital before that and was somehow able to convince a doc (Captain Hawkeye Pierce, I think) to release me. He gave me some meds to take with me and sent me back to my unit.

I was weakened and wheezed a lot but somehow managed to drag myself through the next couple of weeks. Near the end of basic training, there's a grueling fourteen-mile forced march with full body pack, weapons, and gear to a bivouac site where you dig latrines, pull duty, and sleep in two-man canvas pup tents. (This is the Army version of "camping out.")

As a squad leader, during this trek, I was marching at the front of my squad in the company formation. I was still sick, weak, and short of breath. After about five miles, I didn't see how I could make it. Somehow, I kept plugging. **But it ultimately caught up to me.**

In what turned out to be the last mile (I didn't know it was the last mile at the time), I started to fall back and wound up trudging into the bivouac area along with a bunch of other "stragglers." It was embarrassing; I was ashamed. That night, my DI, Sergeant Gambrell, came to me at my tent with some bad news. We had bonded, and I knew he was fond of me. He was well aware of my condition, but nonetheless he said, "Mike, I'm going to have to relieve you as squad leader." (He had always called me and everyone else by our last names. This was the first time he ever called me "Mike.")

Well, I finished basic training on time, got over my pneumonia, and did very well in the Army. As a matter of fact, military service was one of best things that ever happened to me. **I matured in the Army, and after I was discharged, I went back to college on the GI Bill and earned an MBA, and my career took off from there.**

NOW, HERE'S THE BIG FINISH AND THE MORAL OF THIS STORY.

That basic training forced-march experience has stuck in my mind ever since. And I've always wondered if I could have hung in there and kept up the pace for another mile, only about fifteen more minutes. This wasn't like the Bataan Death March. It wasn't life or death. But in essence, I quit. I failed. Yeah, there were extenuating circumstances. But I can't help thinking:

BEFORE I STARTED TO DROP BACK, COULDN'T I HAVE TAKEN JUST ONE MORE STEP (LEFT) AND THEN ONE MORE (RIGHT)? THEN LEFT, RIGHT, LEFT, RIGHT — AGAIN AND AGAIN?

And that's been my "left, right" philosophy ever since. At many junctures in my life when I've faced adversity or setbacks—in my career, my personal life, finances, sports, relationships, you name it—I've said to myself, metaphorically:

"TAKE ONE MORE STEP AND THEN ANOTHER, HANG IN THERE, STICK IT OUT, SEE IT THROUGH, PERSEVERE, DON'T BE A QUITTER."

In the grand scheme of things, that basic training incident was a relatively small setback, but what I learned from it has turned out to pay big dividends for me so many times since.

Having shared this story with my daughters when they were young, I've been gratified and proud to have them relate how they've put my "left, right, left right" concept to good use. **Maybe you can too.**

Mike has been Denver's award-winning, leading radio talk show host throughout his thirty-eight years on air and a columnist for the *Denver Post* and *Rocky Mountain News*. He holds an MBA degree from the University of Denver, was a corporate finance executive at Samsonite and Beatrice Foods, served as special assistant for financial management to the assistant secretary of the Navy at the Pentagon, and is a veteran of the US Army. Mike's book, *Reality: A Plain-Talk Guide to Economics, Politics, Government and Culture*, was published in 2015. He grew up in New York City and has lived in Colorado for almost fifty years.

ANTONIO SABATO JR.

MODEL • ACTOR

I BELIEVE IN HARD WORK AND DEDICATION.

WITH SET GOALS, PERSEVERANCE, GOOD ETHICS, AND PROFESSIONALISM, THE SKY HAS NO LIMITS.

Antonio Sabato Jr. learned the value of freedom at a young age. His grandmother was a Holocaust survivor and taught Antonio the need to stand up for justice. His mother escaped communism in Czechoslovakia and met Antonio's father in Italy. Antonio's parents eventually realized that the best way to provide a better life for Antonio and his sister was to immigrate to the United States legally in 1985.

Antonio was taught the importance of a strong work ethic as he watched his parents work two to three jobs to make ends meet. At thirteen years old, Antonio quickly learned English and became trilingual after studying Spanish in school. In 1996, after completing the necessary steps, Antonio became a United States citizen—what he calls "the proudest moment of my life."

Antonio went on to become a model and actor, gracing the covers of magazines around the world. He expanded his business resume to include successful ventures as a small business owner, restaurateur, author, producer, and race car driver.

Most recently, Antonio decided that, like many of us, he has had enough of professional politicians who care nothing about their local communities. Antonio was inspired to run for Congress in California's 26th district because he wanted to give back to the country that gave him his freedom and opportunities.

GABE SACHS

WRITER • PRODUCER

What is success? Well, if you're looking at success as becoming rich and famous . . . it's a crapshoot. **The odds of becoming rich and famous doing something that you love are not high.** It's not impossible, but a lot depends on luck and being in the right place at the right time.

THERE ARE SO MANY TALENTED PEOPLE IN THE WORLD WHO DON'T GET DISCOVERED, BUT THAT DOESN'T MEAN THEY AREN'T SUCCESSFUL.

People define success in many ways. **My definition of success is creating a life in which you are truly happy in what you are doing.** It doesn't happen instantly, and it requires hard work and tenacity. If you work a job that you dislike but that job funds your path to what makes you happy in life, then you have already achieved success. I worked during the day at a job I couldn't stand, but it got me my own apartment. At night, I spent my time writing as much as I could. And even though I could barely pay my rent, I was writing, and I loved it.

Now if you actually get to the place where you are doing what you love, congratulations. But that's only half the battle. Because if you want to stay there (or continue paying your rent doing what you love), then here's the most important piece of advice I can give you:

BE NICE—PLAIN AND SIMPLE.

Be nice and be generous with your time. People want to be around nice people. I call it the trickle-down theory. **It creates nicer people around you and a nicer environment to work in.** And it makes a big, big difference, I promise you.

Sure, there are a lot of horrible people that are financially successful, but they are miserable. And it doesn't matter how many cars or houses you own—**if you aren't happy, you haven't achieved personal success.** I often speak at USC's School of Cinematic Arts, and I'm constantly explaining that if you start out as being the best person you can be and the most generous you can be in regard to helping others and collaborating with people, you will achieve success. People want to help people who help them. It will all come back to you. Now, if you mix that attitude with hard work, things will pay off. Remember, there is no magic number you have to hit to call yourself successful.

SUCCESS IS KNOWING THAT LIFE IS YOUR JOURNEY TO DO WHAT YOU TRULY WANT TO DO.

Gabe Sachs makes up half of the writing-producing team of Sachs/Judah Productions. Gabe and Jeff Judah have been writer/producers on many TV shows, including *Freaks & Geeks*, *Just Shoot Me*, *Undeclared*, *Life as We Know It*, and *90210*, and they have just finished four seasons of *The Night Shift* for NBC. They wrote the features *Diary of a Wimpy Kid* and *Diary of a Wimpy Kid: Rodrick Rules*, which both opened number one at the box office. They are executive producers on the upcoming movie *Magic Camp* and are currently developing two new shows that will be announced in 2019.

IF YOU DON'T SEE YOURSELF AS A WINNER, THEN YOU CANNOT PERFORM AS A WINNER.

ZIG ZIGLAR

JOHNATHON SCHAECH
ACTOR • WRITER • PRODUCER

My father handwrote these words in a letter to me in 1991:

> "I remember the first time I went up the stairway to the 2nd floor of the house and many times thereafter to apprehend a suspect with a gun or other weapon. (I personally know officers that were shot or injured in some way coming up those stairways.) How frightened I was—if I could just have seen the a*****, I would not have felt as afraid. **It's the unknown that makes you feel that way. I tell you these stories to encourage you with your fears.** You and I chose different professions that both take courage."

I must have read those words a hundred times. I'd say to myself over and over again,

"WHAT ARE THE STAIRS I'M AFRAID TO CLIMB?"

In 2018, I spoke out about being sexually molested on my first film in 1993 by a powerful director in *People Magazine*. I had only spoken privately about it a few times before that.

After I shared my story and it came out, I knew I had climbed those stairs my father wrote to me about. It was the complete unknown, as my father had said. The success it brought me to this point was beyond anything I could ever imagine. **Because I no longer allowed something else or someone else to define success for me.**

AND NOW I'M OFF TO CLIMB MY NEXT STAIRCASE.

Johnathon Schaech exploded onto the scene as one of Hollywood's leading men in *How to Make an American Quilt* and Tom Hanks's directorial debut, *That Thing You Do!* Since then, Johnathon has shown incredible versatility as an actor. Over the last twenty years, he's starred in over 160 Hollywood productions, working opposite some of the most acclaimed and awarded actors, producers, writers, and directors, including Gwyneth Paltrow, Antonio Banderas, Bruce Willis, Jessica Lange, and Bill Paxton.

Schaech recently captivated television audiences as the eccentric movie star in Showtime's hit series *Ray Donovan*, *Chicago P.D.*, and *Bluebloods* and has portrayed comic-book legend Jonah Hex on the first three seasons of DC's *Legends of Tomorrow*.

He stars opposite Ana De Armas in Michael Cristofer's *The Night Clerk* (2019).

Johnathon now uses his national voice for dyslexia, working with Harvard University accredited NoticeAbility.org, a nonprofit dedicated to helping students with the brain-based difference identify their unique strengths and build their self-esteem.

Johnathon has a five-year-old son, Camden, with his wife of six years, internet influencer Julie Solomon.

Happiness

lies not in the mere

possession of money;

it lies in the

joy of achievement,

in the thrill of

CREATIVE

EFFORT.

—Franklin D. Roosevelt

TERRY SCHAPPERT

UNITED STATES ARMY SPECIAL FORCES VETERAN

When my friend Sean asked me to be a part of this book, I was flattered and honored—and my first thought was to write about the importance of never quitting during my almost twenty-five-year career as a US Army Green Beret. But the more I thought about it, that seemed too obvious. **Yes, never quit on what you want.**

Something else came to mind, something that isn't so obvious yet in many ways is just as critical: the importance of **maintaining a sense of humor about yourself and bringing humor to those around you.** A man who can make you laugh when things are at their worst—when you're cold, hungry, and wet and your life hangs in the balance—*that* man is a real asset.

I ALWAYS TOOK MY JOB AND MY MISSION IN SPECIAL FORCES SERIOUSLY. BUT I'VE NEVER TAKEN MYSELF TOO SERIOUSLY.

Terry is a Green Beret, TV personality, and professional actor. He is a United States Army National Guard Special Forces veteran and martial artist as well as a frequent commentator on *FOX News*. Terry has hosted multiple television shows, including History Channel's *Warriors with Terry Schappert* and Discovery Channel's *Dude, You're Screwed* and *Shark Attack Survival Guide*.

SCOTT TURNER SCHOFIELD

ACTOR

When I was a little girl, I felt two truths like lightning bolts: **I would grow up to be a man, and I would be a movie star.** I only learned the secret of success when **I stopped keeping both truths a secret.**

LIVING AUTHENTICALLY, NO MATTER THE COST, PUTS YOU ON THE PATH TO LIVING YOUR WILDEST DREAMS AND MAKES YOU SHINE AS YOU GO.

Once I started living my truth as a man, opportunities to tell truths on screen arrived, and they keep coming. **Now I am everything I wanted to be.** I guess the other secrets to my success are that I listened to myself, even as a kid, and believed myself enough to do something about it—**which was everything.**

Named by *OUT Magazine* as a "Trans Influencer of Hollywood," Scott Turner Schofield became the first openly transgender actor in daytime television with the recurring role of "Nick" on CBS's *The Bold and the Beautiful* in 2015. He is a part of Hollywood's Transgender Tipping Point and one of very few female-to-male actors in mainstream media.

SCOTT SCHWARTZ

PRO-WRESTLER • ACTOR

never wanted to be an actor. Whilst wrestling on tour in California, I was approached by an agent who had seen me wrestle on TV. He told me that he thought I had ability and that I should try to enter the field of performing arts. I took him up on his offer and pursued a career as an actor. Early in my career, I was asked to perform roles involving some sort of fight scene. **I was always up to the task.** Because of my professional wrestling background, I was able to breeze through hours of grueling combat while protecting the person I was fighting from harm. Because of my size, agility, ability to carry out dialogue, and mean looks, I got a lot of roles as a bad guy in films and television.

I was a Los Angeles County sheriff's deputy and was involved in law enforcement in Southern California. During my free time, I make many trips to children's hospitals throughout the world. I focus my attention to child life wards, which treat children with life-threatening illnesses. I visit and sign pictures for the children. My endeavors in child life units really began in 1998, when I lost my sister Beth to lung cancer. At that time, doctors told me that a happy, upbeat attitude of the patient is a key factor in battling this tragic disease.

I THINK THE TERMS *SUCCESS* AND *FAILURE* ARE NOT TO BE SUMMED UP UNTIL THE END OF THE LINE, SO TO SPEAK.

If people are sitting around your funeral with smiles on their faces, saying things like, "This world is a better place without him"—**NOT GOOD. A definite "thumbs down" in the success department.** However, if people are authentically grief-stricken and wish you were still here, **that's probably a W on the scorecard.** I hope that the fact that I have visited and put smiles on and instilled laughter in numerous sick children will mean an elevator ride up at the end of this perilous journey.

Scott L. Schwartz is most recognized worldwide as the Ultimate Bad Guy from his acting career, including *Ocean's 11*, *Ocean's 12*, and *Ocean's 13*, *Starsky & Hutch*, *Spider-Man*, *Fun with Dick and Jane*, *Buffy the Vampire Slayer*, *The Mentalist*, *Castle*, and other feature films and TV shows. Before going into acting, Scott was a professional wrestler under the names of "Joshua Ben-Gurion—The Israeli Commando" and "Giant David," performing in rings around the world.

What most fans don't know is that Scott is really the Ultimate Nice Guy and has been visiting children's hospitals worldwide for the past fifteen years after losing his sister to lung cancer in 1998.

HAPPINESS
is not achieved
by the conscious
PURSUIT OF HAPPINESS:
it is generally the
by-product of
OTHER ACTIVITIES.

—Aldous Huxley—

FRANK STALLONE

SINGER-SONGWRITER • ACTOR

I CONTRIBUTE WHAT SUCCESS I HAVE TO A TOTAL BELIEF IN MYSELF AND MY GOD-GIVEN TALENTS.

believe most people are born with a given talent, whether it be art, music, sports, mechanics, etc. Tapping into your talent is another issue in itself. Me, I was born into it. I was not from a musical family, but I gravitated to it by age five and was working as a professional by fifteen. My regrets are that I didn't study music theory seriously enough and I wasn't a born businessman. **I know of many that have minimal talent but are good businesspeople.**

I played in bands under sometimes terrible conditions for little money for years. I didn't have my first hit record until I was thirty-three years old. It was always the love and passion for music that kept me in the game. Most of the friends that I grew up playing music with quit and went off into what we called the "straight world." Some regret it, others don't, but they didn't have the love and desire.

I DON'T ALWAYS BELIEVE SUCCESS IS MEASURED IN DOLLARS AND CENTS; IT'S MEASURED BY THE IMPACT YOU LEAVE ON OTHERS.

In this world, there's nothing better than seeing people in the audience smiling and enjoying your show with something you have created. **Every time I go on stage, I'm presented with an empty canvas. It's my job to paint the picture of the performance I want to achieve for my audience.**

Grammy- and Golden Globe–nominated artist Frank Stallone has been everything from a street singer to a rock singer to a big band singer. He has composed and published more than two hundred of his own songs.

When his brother Sylvester moved to California to begin a film career, it afforded Frank his first big break into the mainstream. Sylvester's low-budget film, which transformed into one of the most successful movies in motion picture history, needed a group of street-corner singers—that movie was *Rocky*. Frank's a cappella, self-penned song "Take You Back" was one of the film's most unforgettable street corner scenes.

Frank's recordings for the *Saturday Night Fever* sequel, *Staying Alive*, soundtrack received a 1983 Golden Globe nomination for Best Soundtrack and a Grammy nomination for Best Original Song, with his single "Far from Over," which became a number-one hit around the world. Over the last two decades, Frank has garnered three Platinum albums, ten Gold albums, and five Gold singles and has acted in fifty films. One of his most memorable on-screen appearances was his role as "Eddie" the bartender in *Barfly*.

Frank has recorded seven solo albums and has written for and sung on eight movie soundtracks.

A BURNING DESIRE,

TO BE & TO DO, IS THE
STARTING POINT,
FROM WHICH THE

dreamer

MUST TAKE OFF.

Napoleon Hill

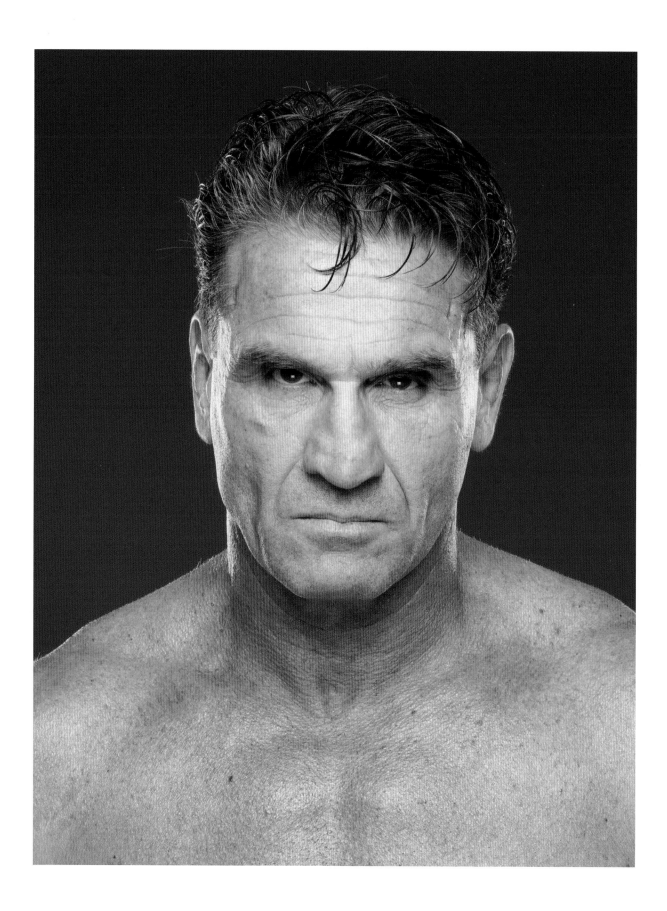

KEN SHAMROCK

MMA FIGHTER • PRO-WRESTLER • AUTHOR

grew up fatherless in a poor neighborhood in Georgia. **I learned life's lessons on the streets.** My mother worked to put food on the table, and I cruised the neighborhood with my brothers, causing trouble wherever we could.

The first time I ran away from home, I was ten. I found refuge in an abandoned car with fellow delinquents but wound up in the hospital after getting stabbed by another child who was also on the run. In the years that followed, I was ousted from seven group homes and served time in juvenile hall. **I had my own way of looking at the world and was always ready to protect my pride with my fists.**

I WAS GIVEN ONE LAST CHANCE TO TURN MY LIFE AROUND.

I went to a group home, the Shamrock Ranch, run by Bob Shamrock, a man renowned for working with misguided youths. Bob had raised more than six hundred boys in his home, and his methods were both unique and effective. In response to the feuds that often arose with prideful boys sleeping under the same roof, he offered them an unorthodox method of resolution. If both parties were willing, he allowed them to throw on boxing gloves and duke it out in the backyard. It did not take long before I was the house champion in both boxing and wrestling. **I never picked fights, but I never backed away from them.** Bob redirected my anger into sports. He got me on a weight-lifting program and enrolled me in wrestling and football. I became the son Bob Shamrock never had. Bob legally adopted me. One day, my father suggested I go into professional wrestling.

Coming from the streets, I wasn't afraid of anything. I very rarely lost a fight, and when I did, I always came back and won.

YOU CAN DO ANYTHING IN LIFE AS LONG AS YOU FOLLOW THE RULES AND STAY WITHIN THE GUIDELINES.

Growing up in group homes, I had learned that **your team suffers when you foul, and your family suffers when you break the law.** I had learned that the hard way.

Ken Shamrock is known as the World's Most Dangerous Man and a godfather of mixed martial arts (MMA). Shamrock is a worldwide-recognized MMA fighter, an inductee into the UFC Hall of Fame, and a former pro-wrestler in the WWF (now WWE).

In addition to fighting, he is the founder of the Lion's Den, a renowned fighting school where some of the world's best fighters have trained. Shamrock has written two books, *Inside the Lion's Den* and *Beyond the Lion's Den*, and has appeared in several films.

AMBITION IS THE LAST REFUGE OF THE FAILURE.

OSCAR WILDE

JERRY SPRINGER

TELEVISION PERSONALITY • TALK SHOW HOST

THE SECRET PATH TO SUCCESS:

First, **be extremely lucky.**

And second, **work really hard** at what you're currently doing.

Someone will notice—and either that will lead to advancement at your present job or you'll be offered other opportunities of which you never even thought.

Throughout an illustrious career, Jerry Springer has become a cultural and civic icon. In addition to Springer's work in entertainment, throughout his life he has also been a lawyer, the mayor of Cincinnati, an award-winning newscaster, author, political pundit, musician, Broadway actor, executive producer, ballroom dancer, and much more. His eponymous show, *The Jerry Springer Show*, just completed its twenty-eighth year in syndication.

The year 2019 brings a new show, *Judge Jerry*, to television screens.

LARRY WALKER

PROFESSIONAL BASEBALL PLAYER

My best advice for my success can probably be summed up by just saying, **"Never quit!"** No matter how bad things look or how bad things are going, it only takes one short period in time for things to turn around! It could be as simple as one game or one at bat for you to realize that **there is something special happening.** That could be what leads you to the Golden Ticket.

As the saying goes,

"QUITTERS NEVER WIN, AND WINNERS NEVER QUIT!"

A simple but accurate saying.

Larry Walker is a seven-time Gold Glove winner, a five-time all-star, a three-time NL batting champ, and a National League MVP. Larry played major league baseball for the Montreal Expos, Colorado Rockies, and Saint Louis Cardinals. He made his first World Series appearance while tying or setting three Cardinals postseason records. Larry announced his retirement from baseball after Game 6 of the 2005 National League Championship series. He is currently active on the baseball Hall of Fame ballot.

MICHAEL WESTMORE

MAKEUP ARTIST

What are the secrets to my success and the steps I had to take to know and acknowledge **"I am successful"?**

SUCCESS DOESN'T NECESSARILY MEAN MONEY AND STATUS;

IT CAN BE ACKNOWLEDGMENT OF ONE'S POSITIVE TRIALS, TRIBULATIONS, AND ACCOMPLISHMENTS.

My roots started at an early age. I grew up by going to work with my hair-stylist mother, Edith, every Saturday to Warner Brothers Studios. At that time, my father, Monte, and all five of my uncles supervised the makeup departments at most every motion picture studio. Each of them was famous for his extraordinary talent and cosmetic innovations. My father's last three pictures included *Rebecca*, which won an Academy Award for Best Picture; *Intermezzo*, with a rising new star named Ingred Bergman; and *Gone with the Wind*.

As a child, I dined and ate ice cream with movie stars—a few names I still recall when dwelling on those bygone moments. For me, this was just day-to-day living since most of my friends and their families were work connected to one or another Hollywood studio. When I was a youngster, my mother taught me to be polite, honest, helpful, kind, and *quiet*. At home and at the studio, I had to follow all the Boy Scout rules. As I grew up, my personality didn't change, only my name; I went from Mickey to Mike to Michael.

Before following in my family's footsteps and having a real job, **I spent my college summers sweeping motion picture stages and the dirt roadway (Appian Way) that lead to the gates of Spartacus**. I cleaned performers' dressing trailers and topped it all off by following an elephant with a wheelbarrow and shovel.

After graduating from The University of California at Santa Barbara with a major in art history, I was hired to be a makeup apprentice at Universal Studios. For the next three years, I was surrounded by famous faces as I was schooled in the art of professional makeup. **It consumed me with a passion.**

I WAS TAUGHT BY GREAT ARTISTS WHO INSPIRED ME TO STRIVE TO BE ONE OF THEM. THESE ARE MY ROOTS.

Michael Westmore is a third generation of Hollywood's royal family of makeup artists and hairstylists. The family's history of makeup and design dates back over 120 years. Grandfather George, who was Winston Churchill's barber, opened his first Hollywood salon in 1917. Michael's father, Monte Sr., was the personal makeup artist to Rudolph Valentino and the makeup supervisor on the classic film *Gone with the Wind*.

During Michael's fifty-plus years in the motion picture industry, eighteen were spent with Gene Rodenberry creating the creatures and aliens that inhabited the *Star Trek* universe.

Michael has been recognized with over one hundred national and international awards, including an Academy Award for the movie *Mask*. He has been honored with nine Emmys and forty-two Emmy nominations. In 2008, he and his family received a star on the Hollywood Walk of Fame.

Presently, he is appearing as "The Mentor" with his daughter McKenzie Westmore on the Syfy TV makeup challenge *Face Off*. He has a recently published autobiography, *Makeup Man*, which is a chronicle of his years of creations from *Rocky* to *Star Trek*.

A man's life is *interesting* primarily when he has **FAILED** ... For it is a sign that he tried to *Surpass* • **himself** •

Georges Clemenceau

TIMOTHY WOODWARD JR.

ACTOR • PRODUCER • DIRECTOR

When I first sat down to write this, I was just going to say, **"Do what you love and love the people you work with."** While I still believe that is a very important element of success, I don't believe there is any one secret key to success. There are numerous key components that have helped me along the way.

We have all heard the saying **"Don't just go through it—grow through it,"** which is so very true and such a simple but important concept. I have personally learned more from my failures than I have from my immediate successes. Failure allows us to identify and unpack our mistakes, accept responsibility for them, and move forward. I am constantly pushing myself to try something outside of my comfort zone and, as a result, **learn something new with each project—whether it works or not.**

DETERMINATION AND PERSEVERANCE ARE INCREDIBLY IMPORTANT BECAUSE NOTHING WORTH HAVING EVER COMES EASY.

There will always be setbacks to overcome and roadblocks to push through. Every time I take on a project, I approach it with the mindset that this is something that I want so badly that I am willing to put in the work and do the best I can.

LONG-TERM THINKING VERSUS SHORT-TERM THINKING IS ANOTHER KEY ELEMENT FOR ME.

There are days when I am so tired and I want to quit so badly, but when I visualize my long-term goals or imagine what my project will look like once it's complete, it allows me to **keep pushing forward.**

From Wild Bill Hickok and Al Capone to modern-day horror, Timothy Woodward Jr. is an American director/producer and cofounder of the successful production company Status Media & Entertainment.

Woodward, who got his start in the entertainment industry on the other side of the camera, began directing music videos before making his directorial feature debut in 2013.

In 2015, Woodward directed his first period piece, "Traded," which released to great commercial success and critical acclaim. It became a prototype for successful indie westerns. Woodward quickly followed *Traded* with the biopics *Hickok*, about the life of Wild Bill Hickok, and *Gangster Land*, a noir thriller about Al Capone and his right-hand enforcer, Machine Gun Jack McGurn.

Often compared to western filmmaking legend Sergio Leone, Woodward continues to create beautiful pieces of art with his director of photography Pablo Diez. Their most recent film and first venture into the world of independent horror, *The Final Wish*, premiered at ScreamFest in 2018.

AFTERWORD

JILL

When you want to learn how something is accomplished, go straight to the source. That's what we did in *Success Factor X*. The participants in this book are leaders and high achievers who were willing to share their stories, tips, and advice. Success is a journey. Always be the student, because there is so much to learn. This book has taught me about myself as well as what some of America's best believe it takes to be successful. Let's take a deeper dive.

One unanimous message: success is not measured by one's bank account. While financial gains may result from one's efforts, not one participant equated success with having more money. Interestingly, many specifically commented that to them, success is *not* about monetary rewards. I believe when you change your mindset to believing that money does not equal success, your success may lead to you having more money. As Darryl McDaniels pointed out on his page, if one acquires wealth from means that are not ethical, we wouldn't consider that success. So, point number one: in and of itself, success and money are not one and the same to the accomplished people in this book.

I also think it important to point out that several participants shared their hardships and challenges. When we see a "successful" person, what we are not seeing is the time, effort, sacrifices, disappointments, and setbacks they experienced to help them get where they are. Most people like to have us think their success came easily. It does not. Thank you to those who revealed a "behind the curtain" look. Very few are born with a silver spoon. In fact, many success stories result from those who used their life challenges as personal motivation to excel.

Another takeaway for me from the participant's advice is: be open. You may have had certain expectations when you purchased this book. Perhaps you thought someone would map out a step by step guide to achieve your success. Success is personal. Learn from the people in the book. When one of ABC's sharks says success is waking happy, think about that. There is beauty in the simplicity of just being happy. How many people achieve so much, work so hard, focus on financial success, and overlook really enjoying life?

Several of the book's contributors took the time to reference or thank someone—a friend, a mentor, a family member. No one accomplishes success alone. Recognize the importance of a good support system. Surround yourself with people who encourage you. I am grateful to my husband, each participant who contributed to *Success Factor X*, and for partnering with Sean on this book. Having someone to bounce ideas off, make you laugh on those days you especially need to, and taking your call late at night or early in the morning goes a long way on the road to success.

Another theme among participants was that several started out in one career or believing they would do or be something, and that isn't always where they landed. Life happens. Things evolve. Plans change. Be open to new adventures and opportunity. Trust the journey and believe that something better is in store.

It is important to understand how *you* perceive success and why it is something you want to attain. For some, success is validation. For others, success is not about winning or being the best at all. If you challenge yourself to run a marathon, even if you are the last to reach the finish line, you have succeeded. Pushing yourself and breaking through boundaries is success. Do not measure or define your success against someone else's. In a large part, success is a mindset. People who see things as either a success or failure, winning or losing, limit their opportunity for growth and true success. For example, would you rather receive a high grade in a beginner class or a lower grade in an advanced class but challenge yourself? Success is in the eye (and mind) of the beholder. When something does not work out as expected, some refer to it as a failure. Others see it as an opportunity to learn and grow, and even as a sign to try a new path. Everyone experiences situations in their lives that do not work out as expected. Do not let those moments define you. Let them inspire you. Use them as lessons and motivation.

I didn't have any preconceived ideas about what the contributors would submit. I was curious to read what they had to say. Everybody has a story and something to teach. When I give a motivational speech, my goal is to have people in the audience hear one thing that day that they can apply to better their lives. The same is true with this book. We intentionally invited a diverse group of contributors with the expectation that everyone reading this will find someone relatable and something that will make a difference in your life.

Success and goals go hand in hand. You need to know what you hope to achieve before you can. When you enter a situation, identify the purpose and what you want to achieve. Afterward, determine if that goal was met and what you learned that can help you in the future. My goal for this book was twofold: (1) I wanted to publish a book that was visually attractive and intellectually inspiring. It needed to be an uplifting book that people could be proud to give as a gift or display in one's home and refer to often. (2) To connect with people. For me, life is about sharing. I thrive on projects that are meaningful and allow me to meet and connect with others. That truly is what fuels me. Please find me on social media, reach out and share what you liked about the book, and what you learned. Let me know what success means to you and if your concept of success is different from having read *Success Factor X*.

Looking forward to connecting.

—Jill

SEAN

The creation of this book came at a precarious time for me. I had recently put several difficult tests in the rearview mirror and was facing several more of staggering difficulty on the near horizon. Whether I knew it or not at the beginning of this project, I was in desperate need of a challenge that would put me back in touch with my inner warrior and quest to succeed. In short order, the universe delivered one in the form of this book.

Compiling *Success Factor X* has been a fascinating journey. Certainly not without its challenges. The most amazing and life-affirming takeaway for me centers on the diversity of our participants and the unanimous quality of their message that true success doesn't lie in external trappings of wealth and power but rather in the ability to inspire and help others while achieving a personal sense of fulfillment and happiness.

I am eternally grateful to both my partner, Jill Liberman, and the dozens of remarkable individuals who have given their time and wisdom toward the realization of *Success Factor X* who have all helped me immeasurably. I am in your debt. My sincerest hope is that our readers benefit as I have.

—Sean

PHOTO CREDITS

SOURCES

Page 3: Winston Churchill, *Their Finest Hour* (London: Cassell, 1949), 541.

Page 7: Confucius, *The Analects*, chapter IV.

Page 13: Walt Disney, as quoted in Pat Williams and Jim Denney, *How to Be like Walt: Capturing the Magic Every Day of Your Life* (Deerfield Beach, FL: Health Communications, 2004), 69.

Page 17: Thomas Edison, as quoted in J. L. Elkhorne, "Edison—The Fabulous Drone," *73 Magazine* 46, no. 3 (March 1967), 52.

Page 23: Edward G. Bulwer-Lytton, *The Boatman* (Edinburgh, 1864).

Page 39: Attributed to Albert Einstein.

Page 45: Ralph Waldo Emerson, as quoted in *Bartlett's Familiar Quotations*, 10th edition (1919).

Page 59: James A. Garfield, as quoted in Tyron Edwards, *A Dictionary of Thoughts: Being a Cyclopedia of Laconic Quotations from the Best Authors of the World, Both Ancient and Modern* (1908), 327.

Page 63: W. S. Gilbert, *Ruddigore* (1887).

Page 67: Bruce Lee, *Striking Thoughts: Bruce Lee's Wisdom for Daily Living* (2000), 121.

Page 73: Edgar A. Guest, "It Couldn't Be Done," stanza 1, *Collected Verse of Edgar A. Guest* (1934), 285.

Page 83: Abraham Lincoln, as quoted in "33 Memorable Quotes from America's 16th resident, Abraham Lincoln," *Deseret News*, February 12, 2013, https://www.deseretnews.com/top/1307/0/33-memorable-quotes-from-Americas-16th-president-Abraham-Lincoln.html.

Page 91: Christopher Morley, *Where the Blue Begins* (1922), 85.

Page 95: Attributed to Leonardo da Vinci.

Page 97: Vincent van Gogh, in his letter to Theo van Gogh, October 28, 1883.

Page 103: Maya Angelou, as quoted in Pauline Edward, *The Power of Time: Understanding the Cycles of Your Life's Path* (Woodbury, MN: Llewellyn Publications, 2007), 45.

Page 111: Robert Louis Stevenson, "El Dorado," *Virginibus Puerisque and Other Papers* (1881).

Page 123: Zig Ziglar, as quoted in "See Yourself," *Ziglar*, https://www.ziglar.com/quotes/see-yourself.

Page 127: Franklin D. Roosevelt, First Inaugural Address, March 4, 1933.

Page 135: Aldous Huxley, "Distractions I," in *Vedanta for the Western World* (1945).

Page 139: Napoleon Hill, *Think and Grow Rich*, rev. ed. (New York: Jeremy P. Tarcher/Penguin, 2005), 27.

Page 143: Oscar Wilde, "Phrases and Philosophies for the Use of the Young," *The Complete Works of Oscar Wilde* (1923), 10:213.

Page 151: Georges Clemenceau, *The Events of His Life as Told by Himself to His Former Secretary, Jean Martet*, trans. Milton Waldman (1930), 220.

MEET SEAN AND JILL

Sean Kanan epitomizes the expression "triple threat," having achieved success as an actor, a producer, and a writer. He is well known for his breakout performance as the villain Mike Barnes in *The Karate Kid Part III*, where he beat out over fifteen hundred hopefuls, his iconic roles in daytime television playing black sheep AJ Quartermaine on *General Hospital*, and his critically acclaimed portrayal of Deacon Sharpe on *The Bold and the Beautiful*, television's most syndicated show in history, which has been seen in over one hundred countries. Sean has produced five feature films and appeared in over a dozen. He is also the author of *The Modern Gentleman: Cooking and Entertaining with Sean Kanan*.

Sean splits his time between Los Angeles and Palm Springs, and he dedicates his free time to charitable endeavors, practicing martial arts, traveling, and learning multiple foreign languages.

Jill Liberman is a sought-after motivational speaker and published author with more than twenty years of experience in the media and television industries. Jill was an active member of NATPE, the National Association of Television Program Executives, and a judge for the nationally televised Cable Ace awards. She has been chairperson and judge for the international Stevie Awards for the last five years recognizing women in business. Jill hosted the number-one rated talk show on WAXY radio and cohosted the television pilot "Thicke and Jill" with actor Alan Thicke.

American Pride, Jill's first book and a stirring tribute to America, received national recognition on television shows, radio, and magazines. The White House had a copy of her book displayed in the lobby, and her story was featured on television as one of the most inspirational women in America. Jill has been featured in numerous publications, including *USA Today* and *Success Magazine*. She graduated from George Washington University with a degree in psychology. *Success Factor X* is Ms. Liberman's fourth book.

Scan to visit **successfactorxbook.com**

Contact Sean and Jill at **contact@successfactorxbook.com**